Commodore 64 Machine Language for the Absolute Beginner.

Commodore 64
Machine Language
for the
Absolute Beginner.

Danny Davis

Melbourne House

Contents

Foreword 1

Chapter 1

Introduction to Machine Language 3
Using a machine language program 4
Memory addressing 4
Summary 6

Chapter 2

Basics of Machine Language Programming 7
The registers 7
Addressing modes 8
Assembly language 11
Screen memory 11
Summary 15

Chapter 3

Introduction to Hexadecimal 17
Binary 17
Why hexadecimal? 19
Absolute addressing 21
Converting hexadecimal to decimal 22
Summary 23

Chapter 4

Introduction to ALPA 25
Summary 30

Chapter 5

Microprocessor Equipment 31
Storing numbers 31
Adding numbers 32
Two byte addition 34
Subtracting numbers 35
Summary 37

Chapter 6

Program Control 39
Sprites 39
Looping using JMP 40
Infinite loops 43
Comparing numbers 44
Relative addressing 47
Summary 48

Chapter 7

Counting, Looping and Pointing 51
Counting to control a loop 51
X and Y registers 53
Using the X register as a counter 54

Using the Y register as an index 56
Summary 59

Chapter 8

Using Information Stored in Tables 61
Displaying characters as graphics 61
Graphics memory 62
Register transfer instructions 68
Summary 70

Chapter 9

Processor Status Codes 71
BCD representation 72
Summary 75

Chapter 10

Logical Operators and Bit Manipulators 77
Changing bits within memory 77
Rotating bits within a byte 81
Clever multiplication 83
Summary 85

Chapter 11

Details of Program Control 87
Program counter 87
Stack control structure 89
Subroutines and the stack 90
Summary 93

Chapter 12

Dealing with the Operating System 95
The kernal 95
CLI 96
RTI 96
Summary 98

Appendices 101

Appendix 1   6510 instruction codes 103
Appendix 2   6510 microprocessor registers 113
Appendix 3   Hexadecimal to decimal conversion table 115
Appendix 4   Relative branch and twos complement numbering tables . . . 117
Appendix 5   Commodore 64 memory map 119
Appendix 6   The screen chip 121
Appendix 7   The sound chip 128
Appendix 8   CIA interface chip 137
Appendix 9   Memory usage directory 143
Appendix 10   Operating system routines 149
Appendix 11   Table of screen codes 165
Appendix 12   Current key pressed 167
Appendix 13   ALPA 169
Appendix 14   Screen codes 181

Glossary 185

FOREWORD

So, you've had your C64 for a while and you've been using BASIC to write programs to do simple tasks. You've slowly been exploring and experimenting with your new computer.

Maybe you've used your computer to run some professionally written software: word processing, accounting systems, educational software or games.

You may have wondered what it is that makes these programs so different to the ones you have been writing in BASIC. These professional programs seem to be able to do many tasks at the same time, including functions which you may have not realised that your computer can do.

Apart from the size of the programs, and the amount of time spent in writing them, the one major difference between your programs and most of the programs that you will buy in a store, is that most professional programs are written wholly or partly in machine language.

Machine language is a must for the really serious programmer. Most games, useful utilities and interface programs are written in machine language.

This book attempts to give you an introduction to the world of machine language, the other side of your Commodore 64.

You will be led through the microprocessor's instruction set slowly at first, practising each instruction learned using the monitor/program entry program ALPA (Assembly Language Programming Aid).

As we work through the instruction set you will meet new concepts and features of your computer, some of which you may not have known it possessed.

You are encouraged throughout the book to check that the computer's output is what you would logically expect it to be. Keep a pen and paper close at hand to copy on paper what the microprocessor is doing to get its answers and to see if your answers agree.

Appendices with explanations are supplied at the back of the book and you will often be referred to these in the text of the book. The rest are provided to give you some information to continue on after you have finished working your way through this book. A list of commonly used terms is also provided if you become confused by the terms used in the book.

The author gratefully acknowledges the assistance of Paul Rosham and Carolyn Sparke in the preparation of the book.

Chapter 1
Introduction to Machine Language

One advantage of machine language (M.L.) is that it allows the programmer to perform several functions to which BASIC is not suited. The most remarkable advantage of machine language, however, is its speed. On the C64 you can carry out approximately 100,000 M.L. instructions per second. BASIC commands are several hundred times slower.

This is due to the fact that BASIC is written in machine language and one single BASIC command may be a machine language program of hundreds of instructions. This is reflected in the capabilities of each of the languages.

Machine language instructions, as you will see as you work your way through this book, are extremely limited in what they can do. They perform only minute tasks and it takes many of them to achieve any 'useful' function. They perform tasks related to the actual machinery of the computer. They tell the computer to remember some numbers and forget others, to see if a key on the keyboard is pressed, to read and write data to cassette tape, and to print a character on the screen.

Machine language programs can be thought of as subroutines — like a subroutine in BASIC — a program within another program that can be used anywhere in the program and returns to where it was called from when it is finished. You use the commands GOSUB and RETURN to execute and then return from a subroutine.

10 GOSUB 1000

10000 RETURN

This wouldn't be a very useful subroutine because it doesn't do anything but it does show how a subroutine works.

Using a machine language program

To call a machine language subroutine from a BASIC program you use the command "Sys address". Just as with the GOSUB command you must tell the computer where your subroutine starts. "GOSUB 1000" calls the subroutine at line number 1000. Similarly "Sys 1000" calls the machine language subroutine at memory address 1000.

NOTE here that memory address 1000 is very different to line number 1000. A memory address is not a program line number, it is the 'address' of an actual piece of memory in the computer.

Memory addressing

You have heard that the C64 has 64K of memory. 64K represents the number of individual pieces of memory in the computer. Each piece of memory can be thought of as a box which can contain one character, one piece of information.

With over 65,000 separate boxes the computer must have a filing system to keep track of them, so that it can find each separate piece of information when it needs it. The filing system it uses gives each box an 'address', which is like the address of your house. You use addresses to find the one particular house you are looking for anywhere within a busy city. You use this address to visit a house, to send it mail or to pick up a parcel from it. The computer, like us, sends information and moves from one place (subroutine) to another using its system of addresses.

The computer's system of addressing is simpler than ours — for it anyway — as it starts at one end of memory and calls it address zero. It then counts through the memory 'boxes', giving each of them a number as it goes — from zero at one end to 65535 right at the other end of the memory. For us this would be very difficult to remember but for the computer it is the logical way to do things. These numbered boxes can be thought of as post office boxes. If you put something in the box at address number one, it will stay there until you put something else in there in its place.

Each box can hold only one thing at a time. When you put something else in a box, what was originally there will be lost forever.

The command "Sys 1000" tells BASIC to execute a machine language subroutine whose first instruction is stored in the box at address 1000.

Using memory directly from BASIC

There are two other basic commands you will find extremely useful in this work.

They enable us to put things in and collect things from the boxes in memory. These commands are "PEEK" and "POKE". Print PEEK (500) picks up the contents of the box at memory address 500 and prints it. This can be used like any other function within a BASIC program, e.g. Let A = PEEK (387) or LET C = 7*PEEK (1078) + 14.

POKE 1100,27 puts the number after the comma, in this case 27, into the box at memory address 1100, e.g. POKE 2179,B or POKE C,X. Try this:

PRINT PEEK (1000)
POKE (1000),200
PRINT PEEK (1000)

We will be using these BASIC commands a lot while experimenting with machine language instructions so that we can find out the results of the programs we write and use. BASIC will be a tool by which we will write, run, and observe our machine language programs.

Machine language as a subroutine

You have read our machine language programs will be used like a subroutine in BASIC. In place of the "GOSUB" we use the "SYS" command.

In BASIC, as you know, a subroutine must end with the command RETURN.

GOSUB 1000

1000 ....
           ....
1020 RETURN

So too our machine language routines must end with a command to RETURN to the main program but it will not be a BASIC command, it will be a machine language instruction.

The machine language instruction for RETURN is ---- 96 ----. That's it, just 96. 96 is what the microprocessor understands as a command to RETURN from a subroutine. It would of course be impossible for us to remember that 96 is RETURN as well as a list of hundreds of other instructions, so we have names for each instruction. These names are

5

meaningless to the computer but, hopefully, make some sense to us, the programmers. These names are short, simple and to the point and are called Mnemonics.

The mnemonic for 96 is RTS. RTS stands for RETURN from Subroutine. Where necessary throughout we will provide both the machine code numbers and the mnemonics of an instruction, as this makes it readable to you while at the same time providing the information the computer needs.

To demonstrate how this works we will create a very **short** machine language program. Type in the following BASIC line:

POKE 49152,96

This puts 96 (the value of the RTS instruction) into the box at memory address at location 49152.

Congratulations, you have just created your first machine language program. It doesn't do much; it is just like the empty BASIC subroutine

GOSUB 400
400 RETURN

Sitting in the box at memory address 49152 is the instruction 96 (RTS).

We will now run it just to check that it works using the command "Sys". Type in the following BASIC line:

SYS 49152

The computer should respond with READY. It has just executed your program.

Chapter 1 SUMMARY

1. Assembly code is fast. It allows access to computer inbuilt hardware functions that are not convenient to use from BASIC.

2. Commands have very minor functions which they can perform.

3. Memory is "addressed" using numbers from 0 to 65535.

4. A memory address can be thought of as a post office box, which can only hold one piece of information at a time.

5. PEEK is used to examine the contents of a memory location from BASIC.

6. POKE is used to put something into a memory location from BASIC.

7. Sys is used to run a machine language program from BASIC.

8. The value 96 (RTS) must be placed at the end of every machine language program to tell the computer to "RETURN from subroutine".

Chapter 2
Basics of Machine Language Programming

Using memory from machine language

So far we have discussed MEMORY, discussed how you can look at things in memory from BASIC, and how to put things in memory from BASIC.

This of course has to be done within our machine language programs as well. We need to be able to pick up some information from one of the boxes in memory, perform operations on it and then return it to the same, or to a different, box in memory. To do this the microprocessor has devices called registers. These can be thought of as hands which the microprocessor uses to get things done.

The registers

There are three of these hands (registers) called A, X and Y, each of which is suited to a particular range of tasks in the same way that a right handed person uses his right hand to play tennis, his left hand to throw the ball in the air to serve, and when needed both hands, e.g. to tie his shoes.

These hands (registers) can pick up information from the memory boxes. Like memory they can only hold one piece of information at a time, but they are not themselves a part of the memory as they have no address. They are an actual part of the microprocessor and there are special machine language instructions which deal with each of them separately.

The accumulator

The first register we will talk about is the 'A' register (or Accumulator). As you will see in the following chapters, the accumulator's functions are the most general of the computer's hands. It is also the register which handles most of the microprocessor's mathematical functions.

In most cases the microprocessor must be holding some information in one of its hands (registers) before it can do anything with it. To get the microprocessor to pick up something from one of the boxes in memory, using the accumulator, you use the instruction "LDA". This mnemonic stands for load accumulator. This loads the contents of one of the boxes in memory into the microprocessor's accumulator hand, e.g.

LDA 253

This command takes the contents of the box at memory address 253 and puts it in the microprocessor's A hand (accumulator). The machine code value of this command is 165 253.

NOTE here that the machine code is in two parts. Unlike the command RTS which is in one part, −96−, the LDA 253 has one part for the command LDA, −165−, and one part for the address of the box in memory which contains the information being picked up, −253−. These two parts of the instruction are put in separate memory boxes so the boxes containing the program LDA 38 would look like:

RTS

165
38
96

Addressing modes

Most machine language instructions have several different forms or modes, which allow the programmer flexibility in choosing how and where he will put his data in memory for his program to operate on. There are eight different forms for LDA alone, called Addressing Modes.

In various different ways, these addressing modes alter the way in which the address of the box in memory to be used is specified within the instruction.

For example, assume you had an instruction to take a letter out of a certain post office box. Your instructions could tell you to do this in several different ways:

1. You could be told to look for box number 17.

2. You could be told to look for the box third from the right on the second bottom row.

3. You could be told to look for the box owned by Mr. Smith.

4. You could be told to look for the box whose address was contained in a different box.

5. You could simply be handed the letter.

You will find out more about addressing modes later in the book, but for now you will be introduced to three of the eight different forms of the LDA command.

Mode 1 — 165 253   LDA 253

This is a short form of the LDA. For reasons which will be explained later, it can only access memory over a small range of possible addresses. This short form is called zero page addressing.

Mode 2 — 173 55 4   LDA 1Ø79

This is a longer form of the LDA command; it can access a box anywhere in memory. NOTE here that the machine code is in three parts. The first part — 173 — is the command for LDA in this three part form. The — 55 — and the — 4 — represent the address of the box 1Ø79 which contains the data to be put in the A hand. The reasons for this apparently strange number which makes 1Ø79 into 55,4 will become clear in the following chapter. This mode is called absolute addressing.

Mode 3 — 169 71   LDA # 71

This command is different from the previous two. Instead of looking for the information to be put in the accumulator in one of the boxes in memory, the information you want is given to you as part of the instruction. In this case the number 71 will be put in the accumulator. It has nothing at all to do with the box at address number 71. This is like example number on page 8. Note here that this different type of addressing known as 'immediate' addressing is shown in the mnemonic by a '#' symbol before the number.

We now know how to get the microprocessor to pick something up from memory, but before we can do anything useful we have to know how to get the microprocessor to do something with it. To get the microprocessor to place the contents of its A hand (accumulator) in memory, we use the instruction STA which stands for Store Accumulator. This puts the contents of the accumulator in a specified box in memory.

This instruction too has several addressing modes (seven in fact) but only two of them will be discussed here.

Mode 1 — 133 41   STA 41

This instruction puts the contents of the accumulator in the box at address 41. As in the LDA, the similar instruction in two parts (zero page mode) can only reach a limited number of addresses in memory boxes.

Mode 2 — 141 57 03   STA 825

This is like Mode 1 except that it can put the contents of the accumulator in a box anywhere in memory (absolute addressing). The − 141 − specifies the instruction and the − 57 − and the − 3 − contain the address of box 825 (this is explained in Chapter 3).

QUESTION: Why is there no 'STA' immediate mode (see LDA # 71)?
ANSWER: The 'immediate' mode in 'LDA # 71' puts the number in the instruction −71− into the accumulator, somewhat like being handed a letter, not just a post office box number of where to find the letter. STA immediate mode would attempt to put the contents of the accumulator in the STA instruction itself. This is like being told to put a letter not into a post office box but into the instructions you have been given. Obviously this has no practical meaning.

Simple program input routine

We will now write a few machine language programs to examine the instructions we have learned so far. To make it easier, enter the following basic program:

```
5       PRINT CHR$ (147); "......"
10      REM THIS PROGRAM WILL MAKE IT EASIER TO ENTER
        MACHINE CODE PROGRAMS
20      READ A
30      IF A = −1 THEN GOTO 70
40      POKE 49152 + X,A
50      X = X + 1
60      GOTO 20
70      PRINT "BEFORE...−LOCATION 1024 "; PEEK (1024)
80      SYS 49152
90      PRINT "AFTER... −LOCATION 1024 "; PEEK (1024)
100     END
1000 DATA 169, 1 : REM LDA#1
1010 DATA 141, 0, 4 : REM STA 1024
1020 DATA 96 : REM RTS
9999 DATA − 1
```

LINES 1000-9999 contain our machine language program.
LINES 20-60 puts our program from data statements into memory boxes starting from 49152 so it can be run.
LINES 70-90 print "BEFORE" and "AFTER" tests on the memory we are getting our machine language program to change.

When the basic program is finished, our machine language program will be contained in memory boxes as follows:

Address	Data
49152	169
49153	1
49154	141
49155	0
49156	4
49157	96

For the programmer's benefit this is written out in mnemonic form as follows:

49152	LDA #1
49154	STA 1024
49157	RTS

Assembly language

A program written out in mnemonic form is called an 'assembly languge' program, because to transform this list of letters which can be understood by the programmer into a list of letters which can be understood by the microprocessor, you use a program called an 'assembler'. Throughout the book we will give you programs in both formats:

address	code			mnemonics
49152:	169	1		LDA#1
49154:	141	0	4	STA 1024
49157:	96			RTS

Our basic program, as well as placing our machine code in memory, runs our program (see line 80).

You will see by our before and after analysis of memory address 1024 that it has been changed by our program as we intended. The original value of location 1024 could have been anything. The number you see **may** change each time you run the program. It is impossible to know what will be in memory **before** you put something in there yourself, just as you can't tell what might be left over in a post office box you haven't looked into before. The value in memory address 1024 after the program has been run is :1. This shows that our program did what was expected — it loaded the number 1 into the accumulator and then stored it into memory at 1024.

Screen memory

There is one result from this program which you may not have expected. Look at the top left hand corner of the screen. You will see it contains an 'A'. Line 5 of the program clears the screen, and nowhere in the basic program was the 'A' printed on the screen, therefore it must have been put there by the machine language program. We know the machine language program puts the value 1 into location 1024. Could this print an 'A' on the screen? Try it from BASIC and see what happens. Press the CLR to clear the screen. Type:

POKE 1024,1

You will see that the 'A' has reappeared on the top left corner of the screen. Ths has happened because memory at 1024 has a dual purpose. It is used to display things on the screen, as well as carrying out the remembering functions at normal memory. The post office box description is still valid, but now the boxes seem to have glass fronts so that you can see on your screen what the boxes have inside them. If you look at the table of screen display codes in appendix 14, you will see that for the value 1 that we placed in location 1024, the character that should be displayed is an 'A'. (SET 1 is used by default. To change the character set being used, press the commodore key and the shift key at the same time.)

Let's try to display some of the other characters in the table on the screen. Let's try to print an 'X' on the screen. First we need to look up the table of screen display codes to find the value corresponding to the letter 'X'. You will find that this value is 24. To put this in memory at address 1024 we will use the program we wrote earlier:

LDA # 1
STA 1024
RTS

But this time we will change the LDA # 1 to a LDA # 24. Using the same BASIC program to put this into memory, we must first change line 1000 which holds the data for the LDA command. This must now read:

1000 DATA 169,24   :REM LDA # 24

Our machine language program will now (when the basic progam is run) read:

49152	169	24		LDA # 24
49154	141	0	4	STA 1024
49157	96	0		RTS

When this is run you will now see an 'X' appear in the top left hand corner of your screen.

At this stage you might ask, how do I print something somewhere else on the screen? The answer is simple. 'Screen Memory' (these 'glassfronted' boxes) exists in memory from 1024 all the way through to 2023. It is set up in 25 rows of 40 columns as you see on your screen. Memory at 1024 appears on the top left corner, 1025 appears next to that to the right, and 1026 next to that. Similarly 1024 + 40 (1064) appears immediately under 1024 on the left edge at the second top row and 1064 + 40 (1104) under that, and so on.

Using the same basic routine to enter our program, we will now try to print on the row second from the top of the screen. The address of this place on the screen is given by 1024 + 40 (screen base +1 row) = 1064.

Therefore we want our program to be:

```
LDA # 24      Character 'X'
STA 1064      First column Second row
RTS
```

To do this we change the data for our program on line 1010 to read:

```
1010 DATA 141, 40, 4      :REM STA 1064
```

The machine language program will now print an 'X' on the second line from the top of the screen.

Printing a message

We will now use our BASIC program to write a bigger program which will write a message on the screen. Type the following lines:

```
1000  DATA  169,8
1010  DATA  141,0,4
1020  DATA  169,5
1030  DATA  141,1,4
1040  DATA  169,12
1050  DATA  141,2,4
1060  DATA  141,3,4
1070  DATA  169,15
1080  DATA  141,4,4
1090  DATA  96
```

Now run the program. You will see that it has printed "HELLO" at the top of the screen. The machine language program we wrote to do this was:

Address	MACHINE CODE			ASSEMBLY CODE	
49152	169	8		LDA # 8	SCREEN DISPLAY CODE FOR 'H'
49154	141	0	4	STA 1024	
49157	169	5		LDA # 5	SCREEN DISPLAY CODE FOR 'E'
49159	141	1	4	STA 1025	
49162	169	12		LDA # 12	SCREEN DISPLAY CODE FOR 'L'
49164	141	2	4	STA 1026	
49167	141	3	4	STA 1027	
49170	169	15		LDA # 15	SCREEN DISPLAY CODE FOR 'O'
49172	141	4	4	STA 1028	
49175	96			RTS	

Check the values used with those given in the table of screen display codes.

It is interesting to note the way in which the two 'L's were printed. There was no need to put the value 12 back into the accumulator after it had been stored in memory once. When you take something from memory, or when you put something from one of the registers (hands) into memory, a copy is taken **and** the original remains where it started.

We can write the same programs we have just written using different addressing modes. It is useful to be able to write the same program in different ways for reasons of program efficiency. Sometimes you want a program to be as fast as possible, sometimes as short as possible, and at other times you will want it to be understandable and easily debugged.

We will change the program this time to give us greater flexibility in what we print. Type in the following lines:

```
15      INPUT "LETTER VALUE"; B : POKE 252, B
1000    DATA 165, 252          : REM LDA 252
1090    DATA 169, 23           : REM LDA # 23
1100    DATA 141, 5, 4         : REM STA 1029
1110    DATA 96                : REM RTS
```

Our machine language program will now look like this:

Address	MACHINE CODE			ASSEMBLY CODE
49152	165	252		LDA 252
49154	141	0	4	STA 1024
49157	169	5		LDA # 5
49159	141	1	4	STA 1025
49162	169	12		LDA # 12
49164	141	2	4	STA 1026
49167	141	3	4	STA 1026
49170	169	15		LDA # 15
49172	141	4	4	STA 1028
49175	169	23		LDA # 23
49177	141	5	4	STA 1029
49180	96			RTS

NOTE that this finds the value at its first letter from the box at memory address 252 using zero page addressing instead of immediate addressing. Line 15 of our basic program sets this box in memory to be any number we choose. Run this program several times choosing the values 25, 2 and 13.

We have seen in this chapter how memory can have more than one function by the example of the memory between 1024 and 2023, which doubles as screen memory. Similarly other parts of memory can have special functions. Different areas of memory are used to control screen colours, graphics, sprites, sound, the keyboard, games controllers (joystick) and many other I/O (input/output) functions. These areas will be referred to throughout the book on a purely introductory level. We encourage you to find more detailed descriptions from more advanced texts e.g. 'Commodore 64 Exposed', Bruce Bayley, published by Melbourne House, and the 'Commodore 64 Programmers's Reference Guide'.

Chapter 2 SUMMARY

1. The microprocessor uses registers (like hands) to move things about and to work on memory.

2. It has three general purpose hands (A(accumulator), X and Y).

3. We use the LDA command to get the microprocessor to pick something up in the accumulator (A hand).

4. We use the STA command to get the microprocessor to put the contents of the accumulator into memory.

5. These commands and many others have several different addressing modes which allow us flexibility in the way we store and use our data:
   - immediate addressing holds the data within the instruction,
   - absolute addressing uses data stored anywhere in memory,
   - zero page addressing uses data stored within a limited area of memory.

6. A program written out in mnemonic form is called an assembly code program.

7. Memory is used to display information on the screen.

8. Information is displayed according to a screen display code which gives a numeric value to any printable character.

9. Memory is used to control other I/O (input/output) functions of the computer.

Chapter 3
Introduction to Hexadecimal

Uses of hexadecimal

So far in this book we have talked about memory in several different ways, but we have not been specific about what it can and cannot hold. We have used memory to hold numbers which represented characters, numeric values, machine code instructions and memory addresses. We have merely had to put a number we want in memory without thinking how the computer actually stores it, in all but one case. It is the absolute addressing mode which has shown us that the computer's numbering system is not as simple as we might have at first thought, e.g. 141 5 4 is the machine code for STA 1029. The 141 represents the STA, leaving the numbers 5 and 4 signifying the address 1029. There is obviously something going on here which we have not accounted for.

We have previously compared the microprocessor's registers and memory to hands. How big a number can you hold in your hand? Well that depends on what we mean by hold. You can use your fingers to count to five, so you can use one hand to hold a number from zero to five. Does that mean the biggest number you can hold is five? You may be surprised to know that the answer is NO.

Counting from 0 to 5 on your fingers like this

is very wasteful of the 'resources' of your hand, just as counting like that on a computer would be wasteful of its resources.

Binary

A computer's 'fingers' can either be up or down (on or off) but, as with your fingers, it can tell which of its 'fingers' is on and which is off. In other

17

words, the value represented depends not only on the number of fingers used but on the position of those fingers. Try this yourself. Give each finger one of the following values (write it on in pen if you like).

Now try to count by adding the numbers represented by each finger in the up (on) position:

Try to represent the following numbers on your fingers: 7, 16, 1∅, 21, 29.

Q. What is the biggest number you can represent on your fingers?
A. 1+2+4+8+16 = 31

As you can see 31 is quite a significant improvement on our original effort of 5. The computer's 'hands' are different from ours in several ways. Its fingers are electronic signals which can either be on or off, as opposed to our fingers being up or down. For the programmer's benefit the condition on is given the value 1 and the condition off is given the value ∅. The other major difference is that the computer has eight 'fingers' on each 'hand'. This may sound silly, but there is no reason for it not to be that way. As it turns out it is a fairly easy setup to handle. The computer's eight fingered hand is called a 'byte' of memory. As with our own fingers, we give each of the computer's 'fingers' one of the following values: 1, 2, 4, 8, 16, 32, 64, 128.

Again we count by adding together the values of all those fingers in the 'on' position.

Eight fingered hand	Computer's 'hand' — byte	Number
	`0 0 1 1 0 0 0 1`	32+16+1 = 49
	`1 1 0 0 0 1 0 0`	128+64+4 = 196
	`0 0 0 1 0 0 0 1`	16+1 = 17

Q. What is the biggest number that can be represented by the computer's 'eight fingered hand'?

A. 128+64+32+16+8+4+2+1 = 255

Without realising it, what we have done in this chapter is introduce the binary numbering system (base two). All computers work in base 2 representing electrical on's and off's by an endless stream of 1's and 0's. This of course would make the programmer's task of understanding what is going on inside the computer even more confusing than it already is, e.g.,

Assembly Code	MACHINE CODE	BINARY		
LDA #8	169 8	10101001	00001000	
STA 1029	149 4 5	10010101	00000100	00000101
RTS	96	01100000		

Why hexadecimal?

This of course would be impossible for a programmer to remember, and difficult to type correctly. We could of course just use decimal as listed in the machine code column. As it turns out, this is not the most convenient form to use. What we do use is hexadecimal or base sixteen. This may sound strange but it becomes very easy to use because it relates closely to the actual binary representation stored by the computer.

To convert between binary and hexadecimal is easy. Each hexadecimal digit can store a number between 0 and 15 just as each decimal digit must be between 0 and 9. Therefore one hexadecimal digit represents one half of a byte (eight fingered hand).

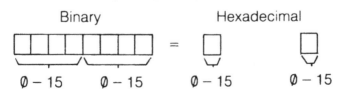

Binary   Hexadecimal

0 – 15   0 – 15   0 – 15   0 – 15

19

The whole eight fingered hand can be shown by two hexadecimal digits. You might be wondering how one digit can show a number between one and fifteen. Well it is exactly the same as decimal but the numbers 10, 11, 12, 13, 14 and 15 are represented by the letters A, B, C, D, E, F respectively.

BINARY	DECIMAL	HEXADECIMAL
0000	0	0
0001	1	1
0010	2	2
0011	3	3
0100	4	4
0101	5	5
0110	6	6
0111	7	7
1000	8	8
1001	9	9
1010	10	A
1011	11	B
1100	12	C
1101	13	D
1110	14	E
1111	15	F
10000	16	10

This shows that converting from binary to hexadecimal is merely dividing into easy-to-see segments of four (fingers).

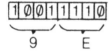
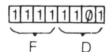
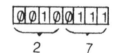

Hex and binary mathematically

Mathematically any base 10, 2, 16 or 179 follows a simple format. Each digit takes the value Ax (BASE) Position-1
In other words in decimal 98617 is

$$7 \times 10^0 + 1 \times 10^1 + 6 \times 10^2 + 8 \times 10^3 + 9 \times 10^4 = 98617$$
$$7 \times 1 + 1 \times 10 + 6 \times 100 + 8 \times 1000 + 9 \times 10000 = 98617$$
$$7 + 10 + 600 + 8000 + 90000 = 98617$$

In binary 01011101 is

$$1 \times 2^0 + 0 \times 2^1 + 1 \times 2^2 + 1 \times 2^3 + 1 \times 2^4 + 0 \times 2^5 + 1 \times 2^6 + 0 \times 2^7 = 93$$
$$1 \times 1 + 0 \times 2 + 1 \times 4 + 1 \times 8 + 1 \times 16 + 0 \times 32 + 1 \times 64 + 0 \times 128 = 93$$
$$1 + 0 + 4 + 8 + 16 + 0 + 64 + 0 = 93$$

In hexadecimal A7C4E is

$14 \times 16^0 + 4 \times 16^1 + 12 \times 16^2 + 7 \times 16^3 + 10 \times 16^4$	= 687182
$14 \times 1 + 4 \times 16 + 12 \times 256 + 7 \times 4096 + 10 \times 65536$	= 687182
$14 + 64 + 3072 + 28672 + 655360$	= 687182

Several points should be noted here. Firstly, any number which can be stored in one memory box (a number from 0 to 255) can be stored in 8 binary digits (bits), or as we have been calling them till now 'fingers'. Any number from 0 to 255 can also fit in two hexadecimal digits (FF = 15 x 16¹ + 15 x 1 = 255). This, however, is where our problem with absolute addressing occurs. If we can't put a number bigger than 255 into memory, how do we specify an address which may be between 0 and 65535 (64K)? The solution is to use two boxes, not added together but as part of the same number. When dealing with addresses we are dealing with 16 finger (16 bit) (2 byte) binary numbers. This is the same as saying four digit hexadecimal numbers. The largest number we can hold in a four digit hexadecimal number is

$$FFFF = 15 \times 1 + 15 \times 16 + 15 \times 256 + 15 \times 4096$$
$$= 15 + 240 + 3840 + 61440$$
$$= 65535 = \textbf{64K}$$

which is large enough to address all of memory, e.g., the 2 byte (16 byte) hex number 13A9 equals

1	3	A	9
0001	0011	1010	1001

$$13 \times 16^2 + A9 \times 16^0$$
$$13 \times 256 + A9$$
$$= 4864$$

For example, the 2 byte hex number 0405

$$= 4 \times 256 + 5$$
$$= 1024 + 5$$
$$= 1029$$

Absolute addressing

If you look back to the beginning of this chapter you will see that this is the problem associated with absolute addressing which we have been trying to solve. One other thing to remember with absolute addressing is that the bytes of the address are **always** stored backwards, e.g.,

```
LDA   1029
= 141   5   4
```

The most significant byte (high byte) − 4 is placed last, and the least significant byte (low byte) − 5 is stored first. NOTE this is opposite to normal, e.g., normally 17 where 1 is the most significant digit (1 × 10) and is stored first. The 7 (7 × 1) is least significant and comes second. For some reason the bytes of an absolute address are always stored low byte, high byte.

This chapter also explains zero page addressing. Two byte instructions leave only 1 byte to specify the address, e.g., LDA   38 − 165 38. We have said before that when using 1 byte we can only count from 0 to 255. Therefore zero page addressing can only address the first 256 bytes of memory. A block of 256 bytes is called a page.

To specify the fact that we are using hexadecimal this book follows the standard practice of placing a $ sign before a hexadecimal number.

LDA   1024   is the same as LDA $400
LDA   65535   is the same as LDA $FFFF
LDA   0   is the same as LDA $0

From now on all machine code listings will also be shown in hexadecimal,

Address	MACHINE CODE $		ASSEMBLY CODE	
49152	A9 8		LDA	#$8
49154	8D 0	4	STA	$400
49157	A9 53		LDA	#$53
49159	8D 1	4	STA	1025
49162	60		RTS	

irrespective of the format used in the assembly code, which will vary depending on the application.

Converting hexadecimal to decimal

We have provided in appendix 3 a table for quick hexadecimal to decimal conversions. To use this chart for single byte numbers, look up the vertical columns for the first hexadecimal (hex) digit and the horizonal rows for the second digit, e.g.,

$2A − 3rd row down
        11th column from left
Printed there is   LO   HI
                42   10752

Look at the number under LO (Low byte). 42 is decimal for $2A hex. For 2 byte hex numbers divide into 2 single bytes. For the left byte (or high byte) look up under HI and add to the low byte LO, e.g.,

$7156   divide HI = $71   LO = $56
HI − 71 − 8th row down
            2nd column from left

```
LO      HI
┌─────────────┐
│113    28928 │
└─────────────┘
```
LO – 56 – 6th row down
                7th column from left
```
LO      HI
┌─────────────┐
│86     22016 │
└─────────────┘
```
Add high and low 28928 + 86 = 29014
$7156 = 29014

NOTE: in all cases
```
                    LO      HI
                   ┌─────────────┐
                   │X       Y    │
                   └─────────────┘
```
       Y = 256 * X

The high byte is 256 times the value of the same low byte.

Chapter 3 SUMMARY

1. In counting on a computer's 'fingers', position (which fingers), as well as the number of fingers, is important.
2. Each of the computer's hands and each piece of memory has 8 'fingers', and the biggest number they can hold in each is 255.
3. An eight 'fingered' piece of memory is called a byte.
4. Each finger has a value which depends on its position. Value = Position -1   1, 2, 4, 8, 16, 32, 64, 128 Binary.
5. Hexadecimal (base sixteen) is the grouping together of binary. 1 Hex digit = 4 binary digits. Hex is easier to handle than binary or decimal.
6. DECIMAL 0 1 2 3 4 5 6 7 8 9 10 11 12 13 14 15 16 17 18
   HEX   0 1 2 3 4 5 6 7 8 9 A B C D E F 10 11 12 etc.
7. Zero page addressing can access the first 256 bits, the maximum addressable by 1 byte.
8. Absolute addressing can access 65536 (64K) bytes of memory (all), which is the maximum addressable by 2 bytes.
9. Absolute addresses are **always** stored low byte first then high byte, e.g. 8D 9817 LDA $1798.
10. Hexadecimal numbers are specified by prefacing them with a $ sign.
11. Remember the quick conversion table for hex to decimal in appendix 3.

Chapter 4
Introduction to ALPA

We have provided you with a basic program called ALPA (Assembly Language Programming Aid) to help you put your machine code programs into memory. A listing of this program appears in Appendix 13. In Chapter 2 we used a small basic program to put our programs into memory but, as you can imagine, this would very soon become a tiresome process. Throughout the rest of the book we have given all our examples of machine language programs in ALPA format. The advantages of ALPA are:

1. Your program is stored as text, and is only stored into the computer's memory in an executable format on the ENTER command.
2. This facility enables instructions to be inserted and deleted without disturbing the placement of other instructions in memory.
3. To help in inserting, deleting and editing, each instruction is put on a separate line with a linenumber which you can use to reference it. (as with inserting, deleting and editing of BASIC programs).
4. The program you have typed in can be listed a page at a time using the LIST command.
5. As you type in each line of the program, the instructions you have typed in hex appear on the screen 'disassembled' into their assembly language instructions, so that you can understand and check the programs as you type them in.
6. You can use the program to disassemble or do an ASCII and hex dump from anywhere in memory.
7. Your program can be stored anywhere in memory.
8. A feature has been included which allows you to refer to other lines of the program from within an instruction using the linenumber. (This will be explained in a later chapter as it becomes relevant.)
9. You can LOAD and SAVE the programs you type in onto cassette for storage.

To get ALPA running

A Listing of ALPA appears in Appendix 13. We realise that it is difficult to type in these programs and be sure that they will work, so we have

25

included an inbuilt, self-test module to check that ALPA has been typed in correctly.

1. Type in the program exactly as it has been listed in Appendix 13.
2. When you have finished typing it in, save ALPA immediately (for cassette save type: SAVE 'ALPA'; for disk save, type SAVE 'ALPA',8)
3. Type: RUN 62000

This runs the self-test part of the program. The self-test creates a 'checksum' for each line of the program and prints it out in the form:

linenumber = checksum.

At the end of the list of linenumber checksums is a checksum total:

TOTAL = total of checksums

There is also a list of the checksums in Appendix 13. If your total is equal to the total printed in Appendix 13, chances are your program will work. If it doesn't work, or if your total does not match ours, you must go through comparing your checksum line for line against those in the book. On lines where the checksums differ, you have made a typing error.

NOTE: 1. If you have made an error in typing in the self-test portion of the program (lines 62000 →) you may not get any output.
2. There may be a bug in the program. Occasionally, but rarely, a correct checksum will be given to an incorrect line. This usually happens where full stops have been typed instead of commas in data statements. This is the probable cause if your checksums appear correct but the program does not work.

Using ALPA

All numbers used in ALPA (except linenumbers) are to be inputted in hexidecimal. When ALPA is RUN, and has initialised itself, it will ask you the question:

LOCATE PROGRAM AT ADDRESS:?

This is asking you where you want ALPA to store the program you will write in memory. As you will see later on (Memory Usage In ALPA), most of our programs are designed to sit in memory at $C000 (49152). Therefore type in C000 in response to this question. If it is necessary to change this, you will be told to do so using the CHANGE command (see later COMMANDS in ALPA). The computer will ask you for input by printing the following line:

COMMAND OR LINENUMBER (###)

At this stage you are ready to type in your program. The programs you will write will be in the following format:

line # (SPACE) HEX Byte (HEX Byte)(HEX Byte)

where — line # is a decimal number between 1 and 199.
— hex byte is the hex value of the command you want to type, followed by 1 or 2 bytes in hex as the operand (e.g. address or data), e.g.,

10 A905

or

20 8D3412

When you type in a line in this format, (errors will be shown), the computer will 'disassemble' your code. In other words, the computer will take the bytes you have typed in and display those bytes and the instructions they represent in assembly language format. For example, if you type

10 A905

the computer will respond with:

10 : A9 05   LDA #$05

This feature enables you to check your code as it is typed in, by reading the assembly language version of your program. For this reason, the programs throughout this book have been written in the following format:

10 A905   LDA #$05
20 8D3412   STA $1234

The numbers you have to type in appear on the left hand side of the line. On the right hand side is the assembly code equivalent, which you should check against the code the computer produces to check that your typing was correct.

The linenumbering system used in ALPA is the same as that used in BASIC:

line ### code
— puts the code on line ### replacing anything previously on that line.
line ###
— deletes line ###

ALPA commands

The following commands are available in ALPA.

1. LIST or LIST line ###
    This command lists the first 22 lines of your program from the beginning or from the line ### specified.
2. ENTER (This is not the ENTER key!)
    This command stores your program in memory at the address specified by the question 'LOCATE PROGRAM AT ADDRESS:?' at the beginning of the program. NOTE you must ENTER a program before you can RUN it.

3. RUN

   This command executes your program in memory starting from the first address it was stored at. The ENTER command must be used prior to the RUN command.

4. WATCH

   This command asks you which address you want to 'WATCH'. The contents of the address specified will be printed before and after the program in memory is RUN. This is used to observe the results of a program.

5. NWATCH

   This command turns off the WATCH feature.

6. CHANGE

   This command asks you the question 'LOCATE PROGRAM AT WHAT ADDRESS:?', and is used to change the storage address without restarting the program.

7. MEMORY

   This command asks you the question 'DISASSEMBLE FROM WHAT ADDRESS:?' It will then disassemble (produce assembly code) using the contents of memory from the address specified for one screen. Any key except M will produce another screen of disassembly. Press the M key to exit to normal command mode.

8. DUMP

   This command asks you the question 'DUMP MEMORY FROM WHAT ADDRESS:?' It will then produce a 'Hex and ASCII dump' of memory from that address. In other words, it will print out the contents of memory from that address as a series of hex bytes, followed by a series of characters which are represented by those numbers in the ASCII character code.

9. LOAD

   This command loads an ALPA program saved using the SAVE command in ALPA from cassette.

10. SAVE

   This command saves the current ALPA program to cassette for LOADing in future to work on without having to type it in again.

11. NEW

   This command clears the current ALPA program, the ENTER address and the WATCH address.

12. QUIT

   This command exits ALPA and returns you to BASIC.

All these commands may be truncated to the first two characters of the command, e.g.,

ENTER can be typed as EN
MEMORY can be typed as ME

NOTE: List is LI but LIST line ### must be typed in full.

28

Memory Usage in ALPA

You will notice that we have, consistently throughout the book, used only a few areas of memory for our programs and our data. We have not done this because they are the only ones which will work, but because we have tried to use memory which we are sure nobody else (BASIC, the Operating System and ALPA itself) will be using.

The programs that run within the computer all the time, BASIC and the Operating System, use specific areas of memory to store their own data in. It is good programming practice to know and avoid these areas to ensure that your program does not stop the Operating System or BASIC from functioning properly. (Remember ALPA is written in BASIC.) By checking through the memory maps and memory usage charts provided in Appendices 9 and 10, you will be able to find other areas to use, but throughout the book we have mainly used memory at:

$C00 – $CFFF
$334 – $33B
$FB – $FE   (zero page)

The best areas to use in zero page memory, when it is very full, are those areas set aside for things such as cassette buffers etc.

If a program written in machine code looks as if it is never going to, stop, it may well not. The way to stop these programs is to hold down together the RUN-STOP and the RESTORE keys. You will be left looking at a clear screen with a "ready" in the left hand corner. You are now in BASIC.

To continue in ALPA with your program intact, type GOTO 2020. This is also the procedure to follow if you accidently get out of ALPA, e.g. by pressing RUN-STOP. If this does not work, type RUN. This should get ALPA working again, but your program will be lost.

When asked the question, "LOCATE PROGRAM AT ADDRESS:?", you should always answer C000 unless otherwise instructed.

We will now repeat some of the programs we used earlier to demonstrate the uses of ALPA, e.g.,

```
10 A901          LDA #$01
20 8D0004        STA $0400
30 60            RTS
```

This is the program we used at the beginning of Chapter 2. To use ALPA, testing location $400 (1024) before and after the program, type the numbers on the left hand side of the program above, e.g.,

```
10 A901
20 8D0004
30 60
```

The computer will print the assembly code to the right of the line. To watch the change in location $40Ø type:

WATCH.   (WHAT ADDRESS)=$40Ø

(If you did not set program location to $CØØØ at the beginning of ALPA, do it now using CHANGE.) Type ENTER, press the CLR key to clear the screen and type RUN. Altering the program is now just a matter of changing the line/s concerned, e.g.,

Type 1Ø A918   LDA #$18
LIST the program now.
Type ENTER, clear the screen with the CLR key, and RUN it.

If we want to, we can disassemble our program in memory to make sure that it has been entered as we expected by typing MEMORY (AT WHAT ADDRESS:?) CØØØ. The listing produced will show your program at the top, followed (after your RTS) by garbage. Press M to exit the disassembly and LIST the program. If we want to, we can save this to cassette.

NOTE: SAVE and LOAD take a few minutes each to do.

Type NEW and try out some of the other programs in Chapter 2 using ALPA. Remember that ALPA treats all numbers as hex numbers (except linenumbers) and that Chapter 2 uses decimal.

Further features of ALPA will be described as they become relevant to the commands being discussed.

Chapter 4 SUMMARY

1. We will use ALPA to enter all of our machine language programs after this chapter.

2. ALPA's commands (which may be abbreviated to the first letters) are as follows:
   LIST
   ENTER
   RUN
   WATCH
   NWATCH
   CHANGE
   MEMORY
   DUMP
   LOAD
   SAVE
   NEW
   QUIT

3. Although we will list programs in the form

   line ### Instructions in Hex Instructions in Assembly Code
   you need only type the line ### and the hex for the computer to respond with the assembly code version.

30

Chapter 5
Microprocessor Equipment

In the previous five chapters we have covered a lot of the groundwork needed to understand the intricacies of machine code programming. More of the basics will be introduced as we go on. We have covered enough at this stage to move on to such things as using machine language to do some arithmetic.

Storing numbers

We know from Chapter 3 that the largest number we can store in a single byte (memory location) is 255. We have also seen that for addresses bigger than 255 we could use two bytes to represent them in low byte/high byte format so that Address = low byte + 256 × high byte.

Surely then we could use the same method to represent any sort of number greater than 255 and less than 65536 (65535 = 255 + 256 × 255), and in fact if necessary this can be taken even further to represent even higher numbers:

Numb = 1st byte + 256 × 2nd byte + 65536 × 3rd byte + . . . etc.

The carry flag

Now, when we add two 1 byte numbers together it is possible that the result is going to be bigger than 255. What then can we do with the result of the addition? If we put the result in one byte it could be no bigger than 255, so

207 + 194 = 401 mod 255 = 145

but also

58 + 87 = 145

Surely there is something wrong here. We must somehow be able to store the extra information lost when a result is larger than 255. There is provision for this within the 6510 microprocessor in the form of a single

31

bit (single finger) 'flag' called the carry flag. The carry flag is 'set' (turned on) if a result is greater than 255, e.g.,

207 + 194 = 145; carry = 1
58 + 87 = 145; carry = 0

NOTE: a single bit **is** large enough to cover all possible cases of carry.

```
    11111111          255
 +  11111111         +255
   ̗1 11111110          254 + carry
  (carry bit
```

Therefore to add two 2 byte numbers together, you add the low bytes first, store the result, and then add the high bytes including the carry bit from the addition of the low bytes, e.g.,

30A7 + 2CC4 = 5D6B

is done in the following manner:

low bytes
```
   A7
 + C4
   6B      carry = 1
```
high bytes
```
   30
 + 2C
 +  1      (carry bit)
   5D
```
Answer = 5D6B

Adding numbers

To handle this, the machine language instruction to add two 1 byte numbers together is ADC (add with carry). This adds the specified number (or memory) to the accumulator and leaves the result in the accumulator. The instruction automatically adds in the carry bit to its calculation. Therefore since the carry bit could be set to anything before you put something in it yourself (like memory — see Chapter 1), it is necessary to set the carry to zero before an addition if that addition does not want to add the carry of a previous calculation. To set the carry flag to zero we use the instruction CLC (Clear Carry flag) before such ADC's.

Type in the following program using ALPA.

```
Locate at ? : C000
10  A903            LDA #$03
20  18              CLC
30  6905            ADC #$05
40  8D3403          STA $0334
50  60              RTS

WATCH
watch what address? 334
ENTER
RUN
```

The program will print:

```
'address 334 before' = 00      3
'address 334 after'  = 08    + 5
                            ————
                              08
```

We will now change lines 10 and 30 to alter the sum we are performing. Type:

```
10  A927            LDA #$27
30  69F4            ADC #$F4
```

ENTER and RUN the program and the computer will respond with:

address 334 before = 08
address 334 after = 1B

```
                        27
                      + F4
                     ————
carry is set →    1  1B
```

NOTE: we cannot tell the carry has been set from our results.

We will now change the program again. This time we will deliberately set the carry using the SEC (Set Carry Flag) command before doing our addition. Type the following lines:

```
10  A903            LDA #$03
20  38              SEC
30  6905            ADC #$05
```

ENTER and RUN the program, and the computer will respond with:

```
address 334 before = 1B
address 334 after = 09
     3
   + 5
   + 1        (carry bit)
  ————
=    9
```

Type the following lines:

```
10 A927        LDA #$27
15 18          CLC
20 69F4        ADC #$F4
25 A903        LDA #$03
30 6914        ADC #$14
```

ENTER and RUN the program.

address 334 before = 9
address 334 after = 18

The carry is not altered between the first and second addition, hence:

```
          27              3
         + F4           + 14
Carry →  11B           +  1 (carry)
                     =   18
```

Now change line 20 and repeat

```
20 6920            ADC #$20
```

address 334 before = 18
address 334 after = 17

```
       27              3
     + 20           + 14
  =  47   carry 0   +  0  (carry)
                  =  17
```

From these we see how the carry bit is 'carried' along from the result of one addition to another.

We will now use this to do an addition of two 2 byte numbers using the method we have described previously.

Two byte addition

Suppose we want to add the numbers 6C67 and 49B2.

```
   6C67
 + 49B2
= ????
```

To do this we must separate the problem into two 1 byte additions:

```
low bytes    67      high bytes   6C
           + B2                  + 49
           1 19                  +  1 (carry)
            carry                  B6
```

34

Clear the previous program using NEW and then type the following:

```
10 A967        LDA #$67
20 18          CLC
30 69B2        ADC #$B2
40 8D3403      STA $334
50 A96C        LDA #$6C
60 6949        ADC #$49
70 8D3503      STA $335
80 60          RTS
```

This will store the low byte of the result in 334 and the high byte of the result in 335. To check our answer we will use the 'watch' command on both bytes (by running the program twice).

ENTER and RUN the program
Address 334 before = ??
Address 334 after   = 19

Now type:

WATCH
watch what address? 335
RUN
Address 335 before = ??
Address 335 after = B6

Now join the high byte and low byte of the results to give the answer:

```
  6C67
+ 49B2
  B619
```

Subtracting numbers

This procedure can be extended to add numbers of any length of bytes.

The microprocessor, as well as having an add command, has a subtract command. Similar to the ADC command the SBC (Subtract with Carry) uses the carry flag in its calculations. Because of the way in which the microprocessor does the subtraction, the carry bit is inverted (1 becomes 0 and 0 becomes 1) in the calculation, therefore

```
      8                    8
    - 5        but       - 5
    - 1                  - CARRY   (CARRY = 1)
=     2        =            3
```

Consequently, to do a subtraction without carry, the carry flag must be set to 1 before the SBC command is used. Type the following:

```
NEW   to clear the program
10 A908          LDA #$08
20 18            CLC
30 E905          SBC #$05
40 8D3403        STA $334
50 60            RTS
WATCH
watch what address? 334
ENTER and then RUN this program.
```

You will see by the results that clearing the carry instead of setting it has given us the wrong answer. We will now correct our mistake by setting the carry to 1 before the subtract.

```
TYPE
20  38     SEC
ENTER
RUN
```

You will now see that we have the correct answer:

$$\begin{array}{cc} 8 & 8 \\ -5 & -5 \\ -1 \ (\text{CARRY}=0) & -0 \ (\text{CARRY}=1) \\ \hline = \quad 2 & = \quad 3 \end{array}$$

You may have wondered how the microprocessor handles subtractions where the result is less than zero. Try for example $8 - E = -6$. Change line 30 of the program, ENTER and RUN it.

```
30 E90E          SBC #$0E
Address 334 before = ??
Address 334 after = FA
```

$$\begin{array}{ccc} 8 & \text{or} & \text{BORROW} = 108 \text{ carry cleared to zero} \\ -E & & -E \\ \hline -6 & & FA \end{array}$$

NOTE: that $-6 = 0 - 6 = FA$
$FA + 6 = 0$

This clearing of the carry to signify a borrow can be used for multibyte subtraction in the same way as it can for multibyte addition. Try to write a program to do the following subtraction:

E615 − 7198

Here is an example:

```
Type NEW
10 A915        LDA #$15
20 38          SEC
30 E998        SBC #$98
40 8D3403      STA $334
50 A9E6        LDA #$E6
60 E971        SBC #$71
70 8D3503      STA $335
80 60          RTS
```

ENTER and RUN this, noting the results. Use WATCH to observe 335 — the high byte of the result and RUN again. Combine the high and low bytes of the result to get the answer 747D.

These instructions ADC and SBC can be used in many addressing modes, like most other instructions. In this chapter we have only used immediate addressing.

NOTE: SEC and CLC have only one addressing mode — implied. They perform a specific task on a specific register, so there are no alternatives to its addressing. Their method of addressing is 'implied' within the instruction.

An exercise

Write a program to add the value $37 to the contents of memory location $334 using ADC in the 'absolute' addressing mode, and put the result back there. Use WATCH to observe the results.

NOTE here:

```
LDA #$FF
CLC
ADC #$01
```

leaves the value $0 in A with the carry set, and

```
LDA #$00
SEC
SBC #$01
```

leaves the value $FF in A with the carry clear (borrow).

Therefore we have what is called 'wraparound'. Counting up past 255 will start again from 0, and downwards past zero will continue from 255 down.

Chapter 5 SUMMARY

1. Any size number may be represented by using more than 1 byte.
   Numb = 1st byte + 2nd byte × 256 + 3rd byte × 65536 + . . . etc.

37

2. The 6510 microprocessor has a carry flag which is set to signify the carry of data into the high byte of a two byte addition.

3. ADC adds two bytes plus the contents of the carry flag. A CLC should be used if the carry is irrelevant to the addition.

4. ADC sets the carry flag if the result is greater than 255, and clears it if it is not. The answer left in the accumulator is always less than 256. (A = Result Mod 256)

5. SBC subtracts memory from the accumulator and then subtracts the inverse of the carry flag. So as not to have the carry interfere with the calculations, an SEC should be used before the SBC.

6. SBC sets the carry flag if the result does not require a borrow (A − M $\geqslant$ 0). The carry is cleared if (A − M < 0) and the result left in A is 256 − (A−M).

7. Two byte addition:
   ```
   CLEAR CARRY
   XX = ADD LOW BYTES + (CARRY = 0)
   YY = ADD HIGH BYTES + (CARRY = ?)
   Result = $YYXX
   ```

8. Two byte subtraction:
   ```
   SET CARRY
   XX = SUBTRACT LOW BYTES − INVERSE (CARRY = 1)
   YY = SUBTRACT HIGH BYTES − INVERSE (CARRY = ?)
   Result = $YYXX
   ```

Chapter 6
Program Control

Sprites

Back in Chapter 2 we saw how we could display information on the screen by placing that data in 'screen memory'. There is a special 'chip' in the C64 which handles screen oriented tasks. It is called the 'VIC-II' chip. (A brief guide to it appears in Appendix 6.) Using the techniques of addition and subtraction that we learned in the previous chapter, we will look at some of the features available on the VIC-II chip.

Type in the following program, using ALPA:

```
NEW
NWATCH
10 A901          LDA #$01
20 8D15D0        STA $D015
30 8D27D0        STA $D027
40 8D4020        STA $2040
50 A932          LDA #$32
60 8D00D0        STA $D000
70 8D01D0        STA $D001
80 60            RTS
ENTER and RUN.
```

This should produce a square blob on the top left of the screen. This square is known as a 'sprite'. It is the size of nine characters but can be moved about the screen easily, quickly and over other characters. It is controlled by the registers (hands) of the VIC-II chip. These registers are similar to the registers of the microprocessor but in order to use them directly they have been 'mapped' onto memory from D000 to D02E. The term mapped means that these registers have been put over the memory. When you access the memory, you are in fact dealing with the registers of the VIC-II chip or whatever else may be 'mapped' over that memory. To use the description of the post office boxes we were using before, you could imagine this sort of mapped memory as post office boxes with false bottoms, with chutes that connect the box to some sort of machine somewhere else in the post office.

Moving the sprite

What we are going to do is write a program to animate that sprite, to move it around the screen.

The two registers which control the position of the sprites (X and Y co-ordinates) are located at addresses D000 and D001. More detail is given about this in Appendix 6. Our program will add 4 to the X co-ordinate register at location D000 several times to move the sprite horizontally across the screen. Type the following lines onto the program already entered:

```
 80  AD00D0        LDA $D000
 90  6904          ADC #$04
100  8D00D0        STA $D000
110  6904          ADC #$04
120  8D00D0        STA $D000
130  6904          ADC #$04
140  8D00D0        STA $D000
150  6904          ADC #$04
160  8D00D0        STA $D000
170  6904          ADC #$04
180  8D00D0        STA $D000
190  60            RTS
```
ENTER and RUN the program.

You will see that the sprite has moved across the screen. It probably moved too fast for you to see it move but it obviously moved. Yet, with all those extra machine language statements, it didn't move very far, and certainly not for very long. How then do we get the sprite to move right across the screen, and how do we get it to keep moving forever? Surely we can't just keep adding more statements? What we need is a command like the basic 'GOTO' command. We need to put the adding instructions inside a loop so that the same instructions are performed again and again.

Looping using JMP

There is an instruction for this — it is the JMP (JUMP) instruction. Like BASIC's 'GOTO' you have to tell the 'JMP' where to jump to in the form JMP address (JMP Low Byte High Byte) (ABSOLUTE ADDRESSING).

We will use this command to create a program equivalent to the following BASIC program.

40

INITIALISE

```
100 X=X+4
110 GOTO 100
```

Type the following:

```
190 ⎫
180 ⎪
170 ⎪
160 ⎬   to delete these lines.
150 ⎪
140 ⎪
130 ⎪
120 ⎭
110 4CL90        JMP L90
120 60           RTS
```

ALPA line number addressing

The addressing mode used in line 110 is not an addressing mode at all, it is a part of ALPA. One of ALPA's features is that it will calculate addresses for you. Normally, when using JMP in absolute addressing mode, you would have to work out the address you want the JMP command to go to — which can be a nuisance as is shown in the following samples:

```
1.  C000 : 4C 08 C0    JMP $C008
    C003 : A9 02        LDA #$02
    C005 : 8D 34 03     STA $334
    C008 : 60           RTS

2.  335 : 4C 3D 03      JMP $33D
    338 : A9 02         LDA #$02
    33A : 8D 34 03      STA $334
    330 : 60            RTS

3.  C000 : 4C 0B C0     JMP $C00B
    C003 : A2 02        LDA #$02
    C005 : 18           CLC
    C006 : 69 04        ADC #$04
    C008 : 8D 34 03     STA $334
    C00B : 60           RTS
```

41

To create program 2. from program 1.

In other words to move the same program to a different part of memory, you would have to go through the whole program, each time changing all the JMP commands that JMP to an address **within** the program, and changing them (and only them) to point to a new address.

To create program 3. from program 1.

This is done by the addition of a few short commands, something you might often do while debugging. You would also have to change any JMP commands to a new address. This would of course be extremely frustrating, time consuming and error prone. Therefore ALPA has a facility for specifying the address of the JMP as a linenumber of the program typed into ALPA (linenumber in the source code). When the program is ENTERed into memory, ALPA converts this reference to a linenumber to an absolute address which the microprocessor can understand.

LIST the program we typed in previously.

```
10  A901        LDA #$01
20  8D15D0      STA $D015
30  8D27D0      STA $D027
40  8D4020      STA $2040
50  A932        LDA #$32
60  8D00D0      STA $D000
70  8D01D0      STA $D001
80  AD00D0      LDA $D000
90  6904        ADC #$04
100 8D00D0      STA $D000
110 4CL90       JMP L90
120 60          RTS
```

ENTER the program.

The computer will respond with:

```
110 4CL90
 90 6904
OK
```

which indicates that its calculation of the address of line 90 (L90) has been done. Type MEM to get a listing of the program in memory:

Disassemble from what address? C000

The computer will respond with:

```
C000 : A9 01          LDA #$01
C002 : 8D 15 D0       STA $D015
C005 : 8D 27 D0       STA $D027
C008 : 8D 40 20       STA $2040
C00B : A9 32          LDA #$32
C00D: 8D 00 D0        STA $D000
C010 : 8D 01 D0       STA $D001
C013 : AD 00 D0       LDA $D000
C016 : 69 04          ADC #$04
C018: 8D 00 D0        STA $D000
C01B : 4C 16 C0       JMP $C016
C01E : 60             RTS
C01F : ?              ?
```

As you can see ALPA has correctly calculated the JMP address.

Now use the CHANGE command to ENTER the program at $334 and disassemble it there. At locations $34F to $351 you will see that ALPA has again calculated the address of the jump correctly without you having to change the program. Now use CHANGE again to return the program to address $C000. ENTER the program and RUN it.

You will notice that the sprite is moving across the screen at speeds that make it blur completely. This is only a small indication of the speed of a machine code program.

Infinite loops

You will also notice that the program is still going. Just like the program

```
100 X = X + 4
110 GOTO 100
```

our program will go forever around the loop we have created. This is called being stuck in an 'infinite loop'.

The RUN/STOP key will not get us out of the loop. There is a machine code program which is part of BASIC which tests to see if the runstop key is being pressed, but our program does not look at that keyboard. There are only two ways of getting out of a machine code infinite loop. One way is to press RUN/STOP and RESTORE keys at the same time. This creates a hardware signal −NMI (Non Maskable Interrupt) which will stop the computer and return it to BASIC. The other way to stop the program is to turn the computer off. Press RUN/STOP RESTORE to stop

43

the program. You will now be in BASIC. To continue ALPA with our program intact type:

GOTO 2020

There is no other way to exit a machine language routine unless it returns by itself using an RTS. Type LIST. NOTE that because of the JMP, the program never gets as far as the RTS as in the following BASIC program:

```
 5  X = 4
10  PRINT "HELLO";X
15  X = X + 4
20  GOTO 10
30  END
```

Obviously the END statement is never reached here either because of the GOTO at line 20.

To get this program to print HELLO 4 to HELLO 100 we would write:

```
 5  X = 4
10  PRINT "HELLO";X
15  X = X + 4
20  IF X = 104 GOTO 40
30  GOTO 10
40  END
```

Here line 20 will GOTO line 40 only if X = 104 and the program will go through to the END statement and stop. If X is not equal to 104, the program will go through to line 30 and continue around the loop to line 10. To do this in machine language we need one instruction to compare two numbers (X and 104) and another instruction to JUMP depending on the result of the comparison (IF . . . GOTO 40).

Comparing numbers

We have previously (see Chapter 5) met the idea of a flag. It is a single bit (single finger) value held inside the microprocessor. In Chapter 5 we met the carry flag which was set to signify the need for a carry in a multibyte addition (or borrow in multibyte subtraction). The microprocessor has seven flags for different purposes which it keeps in a special purpose register called the Processor Status Code Register (or Status Byte). These seven flags (and one blank) are each represented by their own bit (finger) within this byte and have special microprocessor commands dealing with them. These flags are set or reset by most machine code commands. (More will be said about them in Chapter 10.) For example, ADC sets or resets the carry flag depending on the result of the addition. Similarly 'CMP' (Compare), which compares the contents of the accumulator with the contents of a memory location (depending on addressing mode), signifies its results by setting or resetting flags in the status byte.

Branch instructions

The other instruction we said we would need to write our program, is one which would jump to an address dependant on the values of the processor status flags. This form of instruction is called a 'branch' instruction. It is different to the JMP instruction not only in the fact that it is conditional (dependent on the conditions of the status flags), but it is unique in that it uses the relative addressing mode. Relative addressing means that the address used is calculated relative to the branch instruction. More will be said about relative addressing and the way branch instructions work at the end of this chapter. Meanwhile we will use ALPA to calculate the address for us as we did with the JMP instruction.

Zero flag

To test if the result of a CMP instruction is that the two numbers compared were equal, and branch if they were, we use the BEQ (Branch on Equal) command.

To add this to our previous machine language program type:

```
 90 6901          ADC #$01
110 C964          CMP #$64
120 F0L140        BEQ L140
130 4CL90         JMP L90
140 60            RTS
```

Line 90 has been changed so that the sprite does not move as far in each jump, hence the sprite will be slowed down. It will still be moving too fast to be seen. LIST, ENTER and RUN this program.

NOTE: ALPA has calculated and 'OK'ed both addresses using L linenumber.

You will see this time that the sprite moved about halfway across the screen and then stopped as the program ended normally through the RTS.

Program summary

```
lines  10 −  80 initialisation
lines  90 − 130 sprite movement loop
lines 110 − 120 test for end condition
line  140       END
```

We have managed to find a way to use a loop that tests for a condition on which to jump out of the loop. We could however make this more efficient by creating a program that looped until a certain condition is reached. The difference is subtle but it is shown by this BASIC program in comparison to the previous one.

```
 5  X = 4
10  PRINT "HELLO";X
15  X = X + 4
20  IF X <> 104 GOTO 10
30  END
```

By creating a loop until a condition is reached we have saved ourselves one line of the program. If speed or space taken were important to the program, this would be a useful alteration. Overall, it is good programming practice to write code with these considerations in mind. It produces neater, less tangled programs that are easier to read and debug.

This programming method translates well into machine language using the BNE (Branch on Not Equal) command. To achieve this type:

```
120  D0L90              BNE L90
130
```

LIST the program as it currently stands.

Program summary

```
lines  10 −  80  initialisation
lines  90 − 120  sprite movement loop
line  140        END
```

You will see that by changing the loop we have untangled the flow of the program. ENTER and RUN the program to verify that it still functions the same despite the changes. As you can see, there are many ways to write a program. Which is right and which is wrong no one can say, but the better program is, on the whole, the one which is most readable and easiest to debug. This is the most efficient way to write the most efficient code.

There is a lot we can learn by knowing how an instruction works. The CMP instruction for example compares two numbers by doing a subtraction (accumulator − memory) without storing the result. Only the status flags are set or reset. The instructions we have just used (BEQ and BNE) do not refer their 'equalness' to the numbers being compared. They in fact test the status registers 'zero' flag, and stand for:

BEQ − Branch on Equal to Zero
BNE − Branch on Not Equal to Zero.

It is the condition of the zero flag which is set by the result of the subtraction done by the CMP command (accumulator − memory = 0 which sets the zero flag = 1). This flag is then tested by the BEQ or BNE command. This may seem to be a meaningless point until you realise that, since the CMP command is done by a subtraction, the carry flag will also be set by the result. In other words, if the subtraction performed

46

by the CMP needs a 'borrow' (A − Mem < 0, A less than memory), then the carry will be cleared (CARRY = 0). If the subtraction does not need a 'borrow' (A − Mem ⩾ 0, A greater than or equal to memory), then the carry will be set (CARRY = 1).

Therefore the CMP command tests not only A = Mem but also A < Mem and A ⩾ Mem and therefore (if A ⩾ Mem but A ≠ Mem) then A > Mem. We can now write our BASIC program:

```
 5 X = 4
10 PRINT "HELLO";X
15 X = X + 4
20 IF X < 101 GOTO 10
30 END
```

This makes the program a little more self explanatory. It shows clearly that values of X bigger than the cutoff 100 will not be printed. To test for the accumulator less than memory, you use CMP followed by BCC (Branch on Carry Clear) because a borrow will have occurred. To test for the accumulator greater than or equal to memory, use CMP followed by BCS (Branch on Carry Set).

Write a machine language program to move the sprite across the screen using a test for A < memory (as in previous BASIC programs).

Relative addressing

All branch instructions use an addressing mode called relative addressing (JMP is **not** a branch instruction.) In relative addressing the address (the destination of the branch) is calculated relative to the branch instruction. All branch instructions are two bytes long — one byte specifying the instruction and the other specifying the address in some way. This works by the second byte specifying an offset to the address of the first byte **after** the instruction according to the tables in Appendix 4. From 0 − 7F means an equivalent branch forward and from 80 − FF means a Branch backward of 256 − the value. Therefore:

```
      F0 03             BEQ tohere
      8D 34 03          STA $334
tohere 60               RTS
```

will be the same no matter where it is placed in memory.

The value 3 as part of the branch isntruction is the number of bytes from the beginning of the next instruction (8D).

```
1st next byte (34)
2nd next byte (03)
3rd next byte (60)
```

With the following programs, check that the destination address of the branch is in fact the address of the instruction after the branch plus the offset value, e.g.,

```
C0000 : F0 03          BEQ $C005
C0002 : 8D 34 03        STA $0334
C005 : 60              RTS
```

and

```
334 : F0 03            BEQ $0339
336 : 8D 34 03          STA $0334
339 : 60               RTS
```

The machine code remains the same but the disassembled version differs. The program will work exactly the same at either address. This is completely opposite to the case of the JMP which uses absolute addressing and cannot be 'relocated' (moved to another memory address). Fortunately we do not have to calculate the offsets using the tables, because these offsets would have to be recalculated every time an extra instruction was inserted between the branch command and its destination. When we use the branch command we can get ALPA to calculate the offset value for us using branch L linenumber.

Use ALPA to write some programs with branches in them using the L linenumber feature, and check ALPA's output by disassembling the ENTERED code and verify that the branch takes the correct path using the relative branch table in Appendix 4.

Chapter 6 SUMMARY

1. A sprite is a character the size of nine normal characters (3 × 3) which can be moved over the screen on top of other characters by changing its X, Y co-ordinates contained in one of the VIC-11 screen chip's registers.

2. The command JMP address is equivalent to BASIC's GOTO linenumber command. It makes the program 'Jump' to the address specified.

3. ALPA handles addresses internal to the program by referring to them by linenumber, e.g. JMP L40 (Jump to line 40).

4. To break out of an 'infinite loop', press Run Stop – Restore. To start ALPA without losing your program, type goto 2020.

5. The microprocessor's STATUS CODE Register has seven flags (and one blank) which are set by many machine code instructions.

6. Branch instructions jump conditional on the state of the flag referred to by the instruction e.g.

BEQ Branch on Equal		Z = 1
BNE Branch on Not Equal		Z = Ø
BCS Branch on Carry Set		C = 1
BCC Branch on Carry Clear		C = Ø

7. The CMP instruction compares two bytes (by doing a subtraction without storing the result). Only the flags are set by the outcome.

Flags	CARRY	ZERO	Signifies
	Ø	Ø	A < Mem
Value	?	1	A = Mem
	1	?	A ≥ Mem
	1	Ø	A > Mem

8. Relative addressing mode, used only for branch instructions, specifies an address relative to the instruction which uses it, e.g. BNE Ø3 means branch 3 memory addresses forward (see table Appendix 4).

9. ALPA handles this addressing for you if you specify branch L linenumer.

Chapter 7
Counting, Looping and Pointing

Counting to control a loop

Suppose we want to multiply two numbers together. There is no single machine language instruction which can do this, so we would have to write a program to do it. We could, for example, add one number to a Total as many times as the other number is Large. e.g.,

```
10 A = 7 : B = 3
20 T = T + A
30 T = T + A
40 T = T + A
50 PRINT "7*3=";T
```

It would be much easier and more practical (especially for large numbers) to do this in a loop. e.g.,

```
10 A = 7 : B = 3
20 T = T + A
30 B = B − 1
40 IF B <> 0 GOTO 20
50 PRINT "7*3=";T
```

NOTE: this is by no means the best way to multiply two numbers, but we are only interested in the instructions here. A preferred method is described in Chapter 10.

Counting using the accumulator

In this short program, unlike any other program we have dealt with previously, there are two variables. A, which we are adding to the total, and B, which controls the loop. In this case we couldn't stop our loop as we have done in the past by testing the total, because we would have to know the answer before we could write the program. Our machine language program would look, along the lines of what we have done previously, like this:

```
        LDA #$00
        STA A
        LDA #$03
        STA B
loop LDA A
        CLC
        ADC #$07
        STA A
        LDA B
        SEC
        SBC #$01
        STA B
        BNE loop
        RTS
```

Counting using memory

Most of this program consists of loading and storing between the accumulator and memory. Since we so often seem to be adding or subtracting the number one from a value as a counter, or for other reasons, there are special commands to do this for us. INC (Increment Memory) adds 1 to the contents of the address specified and puts the result back in memory at the same address. The same goes for DEC (Decrement Memory), except that it **subtracts** 1 from memory.

   NOTE: INC and DEC **do not** set the carry flag — they **do** set the zero flag.

   We will now write the program thus:

```
10  A903          LDA #$03
20  8D3403        STA $334
30  A900          LDA #$00
40  18            CLC
50  6907          ADC #$07
60  CE3403        DEC $334
70  D0L40         BNE L40
80  8D3503        STA $335
90  60            RTS
WATCH     address? 335
ENTER
RUN
```

Program summary

```
    lines 10 – 30  Initialise
    lines 40 – 70  Loop until Result of DEC = 0
    line  80 – 90  End
```

52

Using INC or DEC we can use any memory as a counter, leaving the accumulator free to do other things.

An exercise

Rewrite the previous program using INC and CMP to test for the end of the loop.

The X and Y registers

There are however even easier ways of creating counters than using INC and DEC. Looking back to Chapter 2, we mentioned that the 6510 microprocessor had three general purpose registers — A, X and Y. Then for the last few chapters we have been talking solely of the most general purpose register, the A register — the accumulator. So, you may now ask, what are the other 'hands' of the microprocessor, the X and Y registers, used for?

And what does 'general purpose' mean? Well, so far we have met one non-general-purpose register the processor status register (there are another two which we will meet in future chapters). The status byte can only be used to contain status flags and nothing else, as compared to the accumulator which can hold any number between 0 and 255 representing anything. The X and Y registers can, like the accumulator, hold any number between 0 and 255, but there are many functions of the accumulator that they cannot do, e.g. Add or Subtract. The X and Y registers are extremely useful as counters.

They can do the following operations (compared to those we have already discussed for the accumulator and for memory).

```
LDA   LOAD ACCUMULATOR WITH MEMORY
LDX   LOAD X WITH MEMORY
LDY   LOAD Y WITH MEMORY

STA   STORE ACCUMULATOR TO MEMORY
STX   STORE X TO MEMORY
STY   STORE Y TO MEMORY

INC   INCREMENT MEMORY ⎤
INX   INCREMENT X       ⎬ IMPLIED ADDRESSING MODE
INY   INCREMENT Y      ⎦

DEC   DECREMENT MEMORY ⎤
DEX   DECREMENT X       ⎬ IMPLIED ADDRESSING MODE
DEY   DECREMENT Y      ⎦

CMP   COMPARE ACCUMULATOR WITH MEMORY
CPX   COMPARE X WITH MEMORY
CPY   COMPARE Y WITH MEMORY
```

Using the x register as a counter

We will now rewrite our multiplication program using the X register as the counter. Type

```
NEW
WATCH               (WHAT ADDRESS?) 335
10 A203             LDX #$03
20 A900             LDA #$00
30 18               CLC
40 6907             ADC #$07
50 CA               DEX
60 D0L30            BNE L30
70 8D3503           STA $335
80 60               RTS
ENTER
RUN
```

This routine is slightly shorter and considerably faster than the original but otherwise not all that different. Rewrite all the commands using the X register, replacing them with the equivalent Y register command. Practise using the X and Y registers in place of the accumulator where possible in the programs in previous chapters.

Moving blocks of memory

How would you write a program to move a block of memory from one place to another? e.g. to move the memory from C100 − C150 to the memory at C200 — C250. Obviously we could not write it as:

```
LDA $C100
STA $C200
LDA $C101
STA $C201
LDA $C102
```

        etc.

This would be ridiculous to even attempt because of the size of the program we would have to write.

We could write the program:

```
LDA $C100
STA $C200
```

followed by some code which did a two byte increment to the address part of the instructions. This is an extremely interesting concept to think about. It is a program which changes itself as it goes. It is called 'self

54

modifying code'. But, because it changes itself, it is very dangerous to use. It is considered very poor programming practice to use it because it is prone to errors of catastrophic proportions (writing over the wrong parts of the program and then trying to execute it will probably cause you to have to turn your computer off and on again before you can continue). Self modifying code is also extremely difficult to debug. It is an interesting concept but **do not** use it within a serious program. Self modifying code is therefore obviously not the answer to our problem.

The answer in fact, lies in addressing modes. Originally we called addressing modes ways of accessing data and memory in different ways and formats. We have so far seen:

Implied addressing

The data is specified as part of the instruction, e.g. SEC, DEY.

Relative addressing

Addressing relative to the instruction — use only in branches.

Absolute addressing

The data is specified by its two byte address in low byte, high byte format.

Zero page addressing

The data is specified by a 1 byte address and hence must be within the first 255 bytes of memory.

Indexed addressing

Our new method of addressing is called 'indexed addressing'. It finds the data to be used in the instruction by adding a one byte 'index' to the absolute address specified in the instruction. The indexing byte is taken from the X or Y register (depending on the instruction used). The X and Y registers are called 'Index' registers.

To use our post office box analogy, it is like being given two pieces of paper, one with a two byte address on it, and the other with a one byte index (∅ – 255). To find the correct box you must add the two numbers together to obtain the correct result. The number on the indexing paper may have been changed, the next time you are asked to do this.

Using the X register as an index

With this addressing mode, our program to move a block of data becomes quite simple. Type the following:

```
NEW
10 A200            LDX #$00
20 BDC804          LDA $04C8,X
30 9DF004          STA $04F0,X
40 E8              INX
50 E028            CPX #$28
60 D0L20           BNE L20
70 60              RTS
ENTER
```

NOTE here that the mnemonic form of indexed addressing has its address field made up by the absolute address, a comma and the register used as the index, even though the following is true:

```
BDC804             LDA $04C8,X
B9C804             LDA $04C8,Y
```

It is the instruction, not the address field, which changes in the actual machine code. RUN the program. As you can see, we have used screen memory again to show that we have in fact duplicated a block of memory. One line on the screen will be copied onto the line below (the 6th line onto the 7th line). Be sure to have text on the 6th line to see the effect!

Non-symmetry of commands

If, as was suggested when we introduced the X and the Y registers, you have substituted the X or Y for the accumulator in some of the early programs, you may be wondering if we could do that here. The answer is no. Not all the commands can use all of the addressing modes. Neither Y nor X (obviously not X) can use the index, X addressing mode being used here with the store (STA). (It is possible to do a LDY ADDR,X but not a STY ADDR,X). For a list of all addressing modes possible for each instruction, don't forget Appendix 1.

Searching through memory

We can use the knowledge we have gained up to this point to achieve some interesting tasks quite simply. For example, if asked to find the fourth occurrence of a certain number, e.g. A9 within 255 bytes of a given address, how do we do it?

The best way is to start simply and work your way up. To find the first occurrence of A9 from F000 onwards we could write:

56

```
                              LDY #$00
                              LDA #$A9
        loop                  CMP $F000,Y
                              BEQ found
                              INY
                              BNE loop
                              RTS (NOT HAVING FOUND A9 from F000
                              —F0FF)
        found                 RTS (HAVING FOUND an A9)
```

We would put a counter program around this routine:

```
                              LDX #$00
        COUNTLOOP             FIND 'A9'
                              INX
                              CPX #$04
                              BNE COUNTLOOP
```

We can combine these into a single program thus:

```
    10  A200                  LDX #$00
    20  A000                  LDY #$00
    30  A9A9                  LDA #$A9
    40  D900F0                CMP $F000,Y
    50  F0L90                 BEQ L90
    60  C8                    INY
    70  D0L40                 BNE L40
    75  8E3403                STX $0334
    80  60                    RTS
    90  E8                    INX
   100  E004                  CPX #$04
   110  D0L60                 BNE L60
   115  8E3403                STX $0334
   120  60                    RTS
```

In this program—when finished, if X = 4, then the fourth occurrence of
              A9 was at $F000 + Y (through RTS line 120),
              —if X<4, there were not four occurrences of A9 from
              $F000 to $F0FF (through RTS line 80),
              —line 110 continues the find routine from the 'INY'. If
              it started from the 'CMP' it would still be looking at
              the 'A9' it found before.

Type WATCH   address? 334
ENTER and RUN this program. The results will tell you whether four
'A9's' were found. Change the program to tell you where the fourth 'A9'
was found (STY $334). ENTER and RUN it again to see the results. Verify
this using the memory DUMP command of ALPA (address? F000).

    We will now change a few things to 'untangle' this program (as we did
earlier in the chapter). Type the following lines:

57

```
40 C8                INY
50 F0L110            BEQ L110
60 D9FFEF            CMP $EFFF,Y
70 D0L40             BNE L40
80 E8                INX
90 E004              CPX #$04
100 D0L40            BNE L40
110 8E3403           STX $0334
120 60               RTS
 75
115
```

As shown before, this 'untangled' program should be easier to follow.
LIST

```
lines  10 —  30   initialisation
lines  40 —  70   Find 'A9' loop
lines  80 — 100   Counter
lines 110 — 120   End
```

(Since Y is incremented before it is used, its initial index value is 1.
Therefore the compare instructions address field has been set back by
1.)

    EFFF,Y (Y = 1) ≡ F000,Y (Y = 0)

ENTER and Run the program. The WATCH function will show you the
results: the contents of $0334 = contents of X = number of 'A9's found.
(The maximum it will find is still 4 — you can change this in line 90 if you
wish).

Using more than one index

We will now write a program using both index registers to index different
data at the same time. Our program will create a list of all the numbers
lower than $38 from $F000 to $F0FF. Type the following:

```
NEW
10 A200              LDX #$00
20 A0FF              LDY #$FF
30 C8                INY
40 B900F0            LDA $F000,Y
50 C9 38             CMP #$38
60 B0L90             BCS L90
70 9D00C2            STA $C200,X
80 E8                INX
90 C0FF              CPY #$FF
100 D0L30            BNE L30
110 8E3403           STX $0334
120 60               RTS
WATCH                (what address?) 334
```

58

X here is used as a pointer (index) to where we are storing our results. Y is used as a pointer to where we are reading our data from. NOTE here that Y starts at $FF, is incremented and so at the first $A9 the Y register contains zero.

To test for numbers less than $38 we have used CMP and BCS (A ⩾ Mem see Chapter 6) to skip the store and increment storage pointer instructions. ENTER and RUN this program. Use the memory DUMP feature (address? C200) to check that the numbers stored are less than $38.

Zero page indexed addressing

All the indexing instructions we have used so far have been indexed from an absolute address (absolute indexed addressing). It is also possible to index from a zero page address (see Chapter 2, zero page indexed addressing). To rewrite the previous program to look through the first 255 bytes of memory (0-255), all we need to do is change line 40 to LDA $00,Y. But, if you check with the list of instructions in Appendix 1, there is no 'LDA zero page, Y' — only 'LDA zero page, X.' We have two choices of what to do here. In practice we would probably continue using the absolute indexed instruction.

    BD 0000   LDA $0000,Y

For the purposes of this exercise, however, we will swap all the usages of the X and the Y, and use LDA zero page, X. Type:

    10 A000   LDY #$00
    20 A2FF   LDX #$FF
    30 E8   INX
    40 B500   LDA $00,X
    70 9900C2   STA $C200,Y
    80 C8   INY
    90 E0FF   CPX #$FF
    110 8C3403   STY $0334
    LIST
    ENTER and RUN

This shows that you must be careful with your choice of registers. Although they can do many of the same things, there are some commands which cannot be done by some registers in some addressing modes. It is wise to constantly refer to the list of instructions in Appendix 1 while writing programs.

Chapter 7   SUMMARY

1. INC — adds one to the contents of memory at the address specified.
2. DEC — subtracts one from the contents of memory at the address specified.

3. The zero flag (but not the carry) is set by these instructions.
4. These are used mostly as loop counters to keep the accumulator free for other things.
5. X and Y, the microprocessor's other two general purpose registers (the first being the accumulator), can be used as counters or as index registers.
6. Indexed addressing adds the value of the register specified to the absolute (or zero page) address used to calculate the final address of the data to be used.
7. Many of the instructions are similar if used on A, X or Y, but there are certain instructions and addressing modes which are not available for each register. When writing programs, make sure the instructions you are trying to use exist in the format you wish to use them in!

Chapter 8
Using Information Stored in Tables

One of the major uses of index registers is the looking up of tables. Tables may be used for many reasons — to hold data, to hold addresses of various subroutines, or perhaps to aid in complex conversions of data from one form to another.

Displaying characters as graphics

One such conversion, for which there is no formula that can be used, is the conversion from screen code to the shape of the character displayed on the screen. Normally this is done by the computer's hardware and we do not have to worry about it. When we are in graphics mode, however, this part of the computer's hardware is turned off. In normal character screen mode, our post office boxes within screen memory display through their 'glass' fronts the character which corresponds to the number stored in that box. That is, we are seeing what is in the box through some sort of 'filter' which converts each number into a different shape to display on the screen. In graphics mode, this 'filter' is taken away and what we see is each bit (finger) of each number stored throughout screen memory. For each bit in each byte which is turned on, there is a dot (pixel) on the screen. For each bit which is turned off there is a black dot on the screen.

In other words the byte $11 which looks like 0 0 0 1 0 0 0 1 would be displayed on the screen as eight dots, three black dots followed by one white dot, followed by three black dots, followed by one white dot. Depending on your television, you may be able to see the dots making up the characters on your screen. Each character is made up by a grid eight dots wide and eight dots high. Since we have just determined that we can display eight dots on the screen using one byte, it follows that to display one character eight dots wide by eight dots high, we would need to use eight bytes displayed one on top of the next.

61

For example, the character A would look like:

8 x 8 pixel grid	binary byte equivalent	hexadecimal byte equivalent

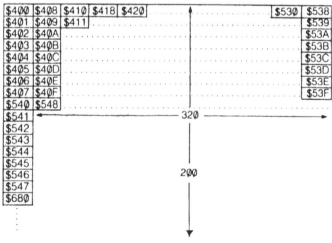

	binary	hex
0	00011000	18
1	00100100	24
2	01000010	42
3	01111110	7E
4	01000010	42
5	01000010	42
6	01000010	42
7	00000000	0

This string of eight bytes — 18, 24, 42, 7E, 42, 42, 42, 0 — is exactly what we find in the 'character generator' memory.

Graphics memory

The memory as displayed in graphics mode does not run simply across the screen. In normal character mode we saw that $400 was on the top left of the screen, $401 next to that, $402 next to that, and so on to the end of the first row at $427. $428 was again the first character in the second row, directly under $400 and so on for 1000 bytes (25 rows x 40 chars).In graphics mode, however, it does not run so simply. Byte $401 is again in the top left of the screen, but $402 appears under that, $403 under that and so on until $407. After $407, $408 appears on the top row next to $401, $409 appears under $408 and so on till $40F; $410 appears next to $408 and so on. In this way the screen memory is defined one character block at a time (eight bytes vertically) across the screen. This goes on for all forty character positions across the screen.

This means that there are forty bytes by eight bits (40 x 8 = 320 pixels) across the screen. It also means that the position underneath $407 will be at $400 + 40 bytes horizontally x 8 bytes vertically = $400 + $320 = $400 + $140 = $540.

The entire screen is 320 x 200 pixels and takes up 320 x 200 ÷ 8 = 8000 bytes of memory. The starting point of screen memory in both graphics and character mode can be changed to suit the programmer (see Appendix 6). In this case, screen memory will overlap with our BASIC program (see Appendix 6). We will actually be able to see the BASIC program (ALPA) on the screen as a series of dots. It is vitally important that we make sure we do not overwrite this program while drawing on the screen.

We have shown that the shape of the character A can be represented by a string of eight bytes. We have also shown that the first eight bytes of screen memory make up one character position. Therefore, by putting those eight values into those eight bytes, we would make an A appear on the screen in the top left hand corner.

Copying the character sets from ROM

Type in the following program. It will copy some of the character sets down from character memory to where they can be more easily used. (Don't worry about those instructions not yet covered.)

```
NEW
 10  A9FE        LDA #$FE
 20  2D0EDC      AND $DC0E
 30  8D0EDC      STA $DC0E
 40  A9FB        LDA #$FB
 50  2501        AND $01
 60  8501        STA $01
 70  A200        LDX #$00
 80  BD00D0      LDA $D000,X
 90  9D00CF      STA $CF00,X
100  BD00D8      LDA $D800,X
110  9D00CE      STA $CE00,X
120  E8          INX
130  D0L80       BNE L80
140  A904        LDA #$04
150  0501        ORA $01
160  8501        STA $01
170  A901        LDA #$01
180  0D0EDC      ORA $DC0E
190  8D0EDC      STA $DC0E
200  60          RTS
NWATCH
ENTER and RUN this program.
```

You now have copies of the first thirty two characters from both character sets at $CE00 and $CF00 (see Appendix 11).

We will now write a program which will look up a list of letters to print, look up the data for each letter, and then print them. First, however, we will write a program to create our message to be printed. Type:

```
NEW
 10  A908          LDA #$08
 20  8D00CD        STA $CD00
 30  A905          LDA #$05
 40  8D01CD        STA $CD01
 50  A90C          LDA #$0C
 60  8D02CD        STA $CD02
 70  8D03CD        STA $CD03
 80  A90F          LDA #$0F
 90  8D04CD        STA $CD04
100  60            RTS
```

ENTER and RUN this program.

We now have 3 tables in memory:

CD00 → Message to be printed
CE00 → Set 1 character
CF00 → Set 2 characters

Several things must be noted in the graphics mode we will be using in the following program.

1. Screen COLOUR memory, which we will mention in Appendix 6, will need to be filled in with certain colours so that the dots we turn on in the screen can be easily seen.

2. We have used a very non-standard setup of graphics and colour screens here both for simplicity and to demonstrate a point. We have put COLOUR memory at $400 (1024) – $800 (2048). Screen graphics memory we have put from $0 – $2000 (8192). Therefore our screen will display data from $0 to $2000.

We will actually be able to see BASIC'S and the Operating System's variables on zero page (see Appendix 9). We will be able to see the system stack (see Chapter 12), ALPA, the program we have typed as BASIC variables, and the values in colour memory. This will all be very confusing to see, especially as each byte will appear as a string of eight dots.

Since we can see these things in memory on the screen, we must be careful not to draw there or we will overwrite this important data. We will be drawing in bytes starting from $400. This, as you know, is also being used as COLOUR memory, so that as we store each byte you will see a character on the screen change colour.

Where will our drawings appear?

Graphics memory as we have arranged it starts at $0 and we are drawing starting from $400. Since each character row is (as we have already said) 40 x 8 = $140 bytes long, our drawing will appear at $400/$140 which is on the fourth character row, eight characters along. We are drawing five characters byte by byte. At eight bytes per character we will be storing 40 bytes. We have said that colour memory coincides with where we will be drawing on the graphics screen memory. Therefore the first forty bytes of colour memory will be altered and the top line on the screen will become a variety of different colors. NOTE also that the screen is cleared by a HOME before the program so that the computer does not scroll the screen to print something when it is finished. This would scroll colour memory also, and our colours would be shifted and the letters we had drawn would be lost at the top of the colour memory scroll.

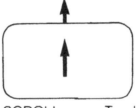

SCREEN   SCROLL   Top line is lost in scroll.

We can now start on the program proper. Type:

```
NEW
 1  A90F       LDA #$0F
 2  A2FF       LDX #$FF
 3  9D0004     STA $400,X
 4  CA         DEX
 5  D0L3       BNE L3
 6  A910       LDA #$10
 7  8D18D0     STA $D018
12  A93B       LDA #$3B
13  8D11D0     STA $D011
14  A000       LDY #$00
15  8C00CC     STY $CC00
16  8C01CC     STY $CC01
18  BE00CD     LDX $CD00,Y
20  A9F8       LDA #$F8
22  18         CLC
24  6908       ADC #$08
26  CA         DEX
28  E0FF       CPX #$FF
30  D0L22      BNE L22
```

65

```
32  A8        TAY
34  AE00CC    LDX $CC00
36  A908      LDA #$08
38  8D02CC    STA $CC02
40  B900CE    LDA $CE00,Y
42  C8        INY
44  9D0004    STA $0400,X
46  E8        INX
48  CE02CC    DEC $CC02
50  D0L40     BNE L40
52  8E00CC    STX $CC00
54  AC01CC    LDY $CC01
56  C8        INY
58  C006      CPY #$06
60  D0L16     BNE L16
62  60        RTS
```

NOTE: this program will leave you in graphics mode. To recover, press Run-Stop-Restore and type GOTO 2020.

Program summary

Lines 1—5   set colours.
Lines 12—13   set up graphics mode.
Lines 14—16   set to zero print position pointer (at CC00) and read character from message pointer (CC01).
Lines 16—18   get character to be printed next.
Lines 20—30   find the start of the data for the character to be printed by multiplying the value by 8 (8 bytes per char.).
Line 32   TAY. This instruction (Transfer Accumulator to Y) merely copies the contents of the accumulator into the Y register (see further later in this chapter).
Lines 36—38   set up a counter to limit the data copying at $CC02.
Lines 40—50   copy the data from its place in the table to its place on the screen, indexing both pointers as it goes.
Line 52   saves the pointer to where we are printing on the screen for use by the next character ($CC00).
Lines 54—60   increment the pointer to the list of letters which make up our message and loop back to print the next, unless they have all been printed.
Line 62   END
ENTER Press CLR and RUN this program.

You will notice that it has printed our message 'HELLO' near the top left hand corner of the screen.

Indirect indexed addressing

There will be some cases where you may be unsure as to which table you want to find your data in. In other words, imagine a program which lets you decide whether you wanted to print the message in upper or lower case letters after the program had run. You will want to use one of the two tables decided on midway through the program. This could be done by having two nearly identical programs, each accessing a different table in memory and having the beginning of the program decide which of the two to use. Of course, this is wasteful of memory. To access data by this method, there is an addressing mode called indirect indexed addressing, which allows you even greater flexibility as to where you must place your data. Indirect indexed addressing is just like absolute indexed addressing, except that the absolute address is not part of the instruction but is held in two successive zero page locations as pointed to by the indirect indexed instruction. In other words, the contents of the zero page address pointed to by the indirect indexed instruction, is the low byte of a low byte/high byte pair which contains an address which is then indexed by the index register Y to obtain the final address. (Indirect indexed addressing is always indexed using the Y register.)

Imagine the following situation, using our post office box analogy. You are handed an instruction to look in a box (zero page). The number you find in that box and the box next to it, go together to make an absolute address (low byte/high byte format). You are then told to add an index (Y) to this address to find the address you are looking for.

The mnemonic for this addressing mode is QQQ (ZP),Y
where QQQ is an instruction, e.g. LDA
      ZP is a one byte zero page address
and the Y is outside the brackets to signify that the indirection is taken first, and the indexed added later.

The upper case/lower case program would, therefore, only store the start address of the correct table in the zero page addresses and call this general purpose routine.

We will now alter our program to do this. Type:

4Ø	B1FD	LDA ($FD),Y
8	A9CF	LDA #$CF
9	85FE	STA $FE
1Ø	A9ØØ	LDA #$ØØ
11	85FD	STA $FD

LIST
ENTER and RUN this program.
Press RUNSTOP-RESTORE to exit, GOTO 2Ø2Ø.

Now by only changing the LDA line 8 to 8 A9CE LDA #$CE, this same program will now change case. Type in line 8 and ENTER and RUN it.

67

Just for interest sake, change line 8 to load a value which is not $CE or $CF, e.g. $47. This will make the program look for its data at some address other than where we placed our character data. NOTE that the program will still work, but what it prints out will be meaningless. The computer cannot tell the difference between meaningful and meaningless data.

Register transfer instructions

Back in line 32 of our program, we snuck in an instruction which you hadn't previously met — TAY (Transfer A into Y). This is only one of a group of quite simple instructions used to copy the contents of one register into another.

The available instructions are:

TAX   (Transfer A into X)
TAY   (Transfer A into Y)
TXA   (Transfer X into A)
TYA   (Transfer Y into A)

These instructions are used mainly when the operations performed on a counter or index require mathematical manipulations that must be done in the accumulator and then returned to the index register.

NOTE: there is **no** instruction to transfer between X and Y. If necessary this must be done through A.

There are two addressing modes we have not yet covered which we will briefly touch on here. The first is called Indexed Indirect Addressing. No, it is not the one we have just covered, that was Indirect Indexed Addressing. The order of the words explains the order of the operations. Previously we saw indirect indexed in the form QQQ (ZP),Y, where the indirection was performed first followed by the indexing. In indexed indirect, QQQ (ZP,X), the indexing is done first to calculate the zero page address which contains the first byte of a two byte address (low byte/high byte format), which is the eventual destination of the instruction.

Imagine that you had a table of addresses in zero page. These addresses point to data or separate tables in memory. To find the first byte of these tables, you would use this instruction to index through the zero page table and use the correct address to find the data from the table you were looking for. In terms of post office boxes, we are saying here is the number of a post office box (zero page). Add to that address the value of the indexing byte (X register). From that calculated address, and from the box next to it (low byte/high byte), we create the address which we will use to find the data we want to work on.

Indirect addressing

The last addressing mode we will cover is called Indirect Addressing. There is only one instruction which uses indirect addressing and that is the JMP command.

The JMP command using absolute addressing 'Jumps' the program to the address specified in the instruction (like GOTO in BASIC).

In indirect addressing, 'JMP (Addr)', the two byte (absolute) address within the brackets is used to point to an address anywhere within memory which holds the low byte of a two byte address which is the destination of the instruction. In other words, the instruction points to an address that, with the next address in memory, specifies the destination of the jump. In post office box terms, this means that you are handed the number of a box. You look in that box and the box next to it to piece together (low byte/high byte format) the address which the JMP instruction will use. The major use of this instruction is in what is known as vectored input or output. For example, if you write a program which jumps directly to the ROM output character address to print a character, and you then want the output to be sent to the disk instead, you would have to change the JMP instruction. Using the vectored output, the program does a JMP indirect on a RAM memory location. If the disk operating system is told to take control of output, it sets up the vector locations so a JMP indirect will go to its programs. If output is directed to the screen, those memory locations will hold the address of the ROM printing routines, and your program will output through there. Here is a list of different addressing modes available on the 6510:

Implied		QQQ
Absolute		QQQ addr
Zero page		QQQ ZP
Immediate		QQQ # byte
Relative		BQQ Byte — (L # from ALPA)
	Absolute X	QQQ addr,X
Indexed	Absolute, Y	QQQ addr,Y
	Zero page,X	QQQ ZP,X
	Zero page,Y	QQQ ZP,Y
Indirect indexed		QQQ (ZP),Y
Indexed indirect		QQQ (ZP,X)
Indirect		JMP (addr)
also		
Accumulator		QQQ A

(An operation performed on the accumulator, see Chapter 10.)

Chapter 8   SUMMARY

1. In graphics mode you can 'see' the contents of screen memory. 1 bit means 1 pixel (dot on screen).

2. Characters are defined within 8 pixel by 8 pixel blocks.

3. Screen memory in graphics mode runs in character blocks, then across the screen line by line.

4. Character sets are stored in ROM 'switched in' over memory from $D000 onwards.

5. Index registers are used to look up tables (among other things), using several indexed addressing modes.

6. In normal indexed addressing, the index register is added to an absolute (or zero page) address to calculate the eventual address.

7. In indirect indexed addressing, the eventual address is calculated by adding the Y register to the 2 byte address stored in the zero page locations pointed to by the 1 byte address in the instruction.

8. In indexed indirect addressing, the eventual address is calculated by adding the X register to the zero page address which forms part of the instruction. The contents of these two zero page locations specify the address.

9. The computer cannot tell the difference between meaningful and meaningless data.

10. TAX, TAY, TXA and TYA are used to transfer data between the index registers and the accumulator.

11. Indirect addressing (for JMP only) uses the contents of two bytes (next to each other), anywhere in memory, as the destination address for the jump.

Chapter 9
Processor Status Codes

We mentioned in Chapters 5 and 6 the concepts of flags within the microprocessor. We talked about the carry flag and the zero flag, and we discussed the branch instructions and other instructions associated with them, e.g. SEC, CLC, BCS, BCC, BEQ and BCC. We said that these flags, along with several others, were stored in a special purpose register within the microprocessor called the processor status code register or, simply, the status register. This register is set out, like any other register or byte in memory, in eight bits (fingers). Each bit represents a flag for a different purpose:

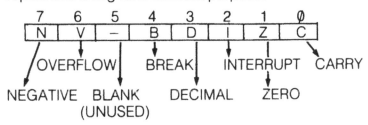

A list of which instructions set which flags can be seen in the table in Appendix 1.

1. **The carry (C) flag,** as we have already seen, is set or cleared to indicate a 'carry' or 'borrow' from the eight bit of the byte into the 'ninth' bit. Since there is no ninth bit, it goes into the carry to be included in future calculations or to be ignored. The carry can be set and cleared using SEC or CLC respectively. A program can test for carry set or cleared using BCS or BCC respectively.

2. **The zero (Z) flag**, as we have already seen, is set or cleared depending on the result of an operation, comparison or transfer of data (Load or Store). A program can test for zero set or cleared by using BEQ or BNE respectively.

3. **Setting the break (B) flag** using the BRK command causes what is known as an interrupt. More will be said about interrupts in Chapter 11. Using a BRK command will cause your machine language program to stop and the computer to jump indirect on the contents of

$FFFE and $FFFF. These ROM addresses hold the address of a break routine which will return you to BASIC. Using the BRK command is a very effective way of debugging a program. By inserting this command into your program at specific points, you will be able to trace (by whether the program stops or hangs) how far a program is getting before it is doing the wrong thing. This instruction gives you a chance to stop a program and test its variables in memory to see if they are what you would expect at this point in the program. Use the BRK command within one of the programs from Chapter 7 to practise using it as a debugging tool.

4. **The interrupt (I) flag** may be set or cleared using SEI and CLI respectively. When set, the interrupt flag will disable certain types of interrupts from occurring (see Chapter 11).

5. **The decimal (D) flag** may be set or cleared using the SED and CLD commands respectively. When the decimal flag is set, the microprocessor goes into decimal or BCD mode. BCD stands for Binary Coded Decimal and is a method of representing decimal numbers within the computer's memory. In the BCD representation, hexadecimal digits 0 – 9 are read as their decimal equivalents and the digits A – F have no meaning. In other words,

BCD REPRESENTATION

Binary	Hex	Decimal value of BCD
00000000	00	0
00000001	01	1
00000010	02	2
00000011	03	3
00000100	04	4
00000101	05	5
00000110	06	6
00000111	07	7
00001000	08	8
00001001	09	9
00010000	10	10
00010001	11	11
00100010	22	22
01000011	43	43
10011000	98	98

This shows that there are six possible codes between the values of 9 and 10 which are wasted.

In decimal mode the microprocessor automatically adds and subtracts BCD numbers, e.g.

Decimal Flag = 0	Decimal Flag = 1
17	17
+26	+26
3D	43

The problems with decimal mode are that it is wasteful of memory and it is very slow to use mathematically (apart from adds and subtracts). On the whole it is easier to use hex and convert for output, and so decimal mode is rarely used. Convert some of the programs in Chapter 5 to work in decimal mode and compare their output to normal calculations.

6. **The negative flag**. So far we have said that the only numbers that could be held within a single byte were those between 0 and 255. We have talked about having to deal with numbers bigger than 255 by using two bytes, but we have not mentioned anything about numbers less than zero. We have used them briefly without realising it back in Chapter 6. We have seen from our use of numbers from 0 — 255 to represent anything from numbers to addresses, from characters to BCD numbers, that the microprocessor will behave the same no matter how we use these numbers. The memory might be a character or an address or an instruction, but if we add one to it the microprocessor will not care what it is we are representing. It will just do it blindly. In Chapter 6 we took our number between 0 and 255 and chose to use it as the value of a relative branch; we chose $00 to $7F as a forward (positive) and $80 to $FF as a backward (negative) branch. This numbering system is purely arbitrary but, as it turns out, it is mathematically sound to use it for representing positive and negative numbers. The system we use is called Two's Complement Arithmetic. We can use the table in Appendix 00 to convert between normal numbers and two's complement numbers, looking for the number in decimal in the centre and finding the correct two's complement hex value on the outside. Mathematically, we take the complement of the binary number (all 1's become 0's and all 0's become 1's) and then add 1, e.g.

COMPLEMENT

$$3 = 0\ 0\ 0\ 0\ 0\ 0\ 1\ 1 \rightarrow \boxed{1|1|1|1|1|1|0|0}$$
$$+1$$
$$= \boxed{1|1|1|1|1|1|0|1} = FD = -3$$

Using this representation, you will see that any byte whose value is greater than 127 (with its high bit, bit 7, turned on) represents a negative number, and any value less than 128 (high bit turned off) represents a positive number.

1 X X X X X X X — NEGATIVE
0 X X X X X X X — POSITIVE

The negative flag in the status register is automatically set (like the zero flag) if any number used as a result of an operation, a comparison or a transfer, is negative. Since the microprocessor cannot tell if a value it is dealing with represents a number or a character or anything else, it always sets the negative flag, if the high bit of the byte being used is set. In other words, the negative flag is always a copy of bit 7 (the high bit) of

73

the result of an operation.

Since the high bit of the byte is a sign bit (representing the sign of the number) we are left with only seven bits to store the actual number. With seven bits you can represent any number between Ø and 127 but, since Ø = −Ø, on the negative side we add one. So two's complement numbers can represent any number from −128 to +127 using one byte.

Let's try some mathematics using our new numbering system.

Two's Complement Binary   Decimal value

Positive + Positive (no different no normal)
```
 ØØØØØ111                        +  7
+ØØØØ1ØØ1                        ++ 9
─────────                       ──────
 ØØØ1ØØØØ                        16   C = Ø V = Ø N = Ø
─────────                       ──────
```

Positive + Negative (negative result)
```
 ØØØØØ111                        +  7
+11110100                       +−12
─────────                       ──────
 11111Ø11                        − 5   C = Ø V = Ø N = 1
─────────                       ──────
```

Positive + Negative (positive result)
```
  ØØØØØ111                       +  7
 +11111101                      +−  3
─────────                       ──────
(1)ØØØØØ1ØØ                      + 4   C = 1 V = Ø N = Ø
─────────                       ──────
```

Positive + Positive (answer greater than 127)
```
 Ø111ØØ11                         115
+ØØ11ØØØ1                        +  49
─────────                       ──────
 1Ø1ØØ1ØØ                        −92   C = Ø V = 1 N = 1
─────────                       ──────
```
                              NOTE: this answer is **wrong!**

Two's complement numbering seems to handle positive and negative numbers well, except in our last example. We said previously that two's complement could only hold numbers from −128 to +127. The answer to our question should have been 164. As in Chapter 3, to hold a number bigger than 255 we needed two bytes, here also we must use two bytes. In normal binary a carry from bit 7 (the high bit) into the high byte was done through the carry. In two's complement we have seven bits and a sign bit so the high bit is bit 6. The microprocessor, not knowing we are using two's complement arithmetic, has as usual 'carried' bit 6 into bit 7. To enable us to correct this, it has set the overflow flag to tell us that this has happened.

7. **The overflow flag.** This flag is set by a carry from bit 6 to bit 7.

7 6 5 4 3 2 1 0

e.g. | 0 | 1 | 1 | 1 | 1 | 1 | 1 | 1 | + | 0 | 0 | 0 | 0 | 0 | 0 | 0 | 1 | = | 1 | 0 | 0 | 0 | 0 | 0 | 0 | 0 |

     127   +   1   =   128

The major use of the overflow flag is in signalling the accidental changing of sign caused by an 'overflow' using two's complement arithmetic. To correct for this accidental change of signs, the sign bit (bit 7) must be complemented (inverted) and a one carried on to a high byte if necessary.

This would make our previously wrong result of −92 (10100100) become 1 x 128 (high byte) + 36 (00100100). 128 + 36 = 164 which is the correct answer.

A program can test for the negative flag being set or cleared using BMI (Branch on Minus) or BPL (Branch on Plus) respectively.

A program can test for the overflow flag being set or cleared using BVS (Branch on Overflow Set) or BVC (Branch on Overflow Clear) respectively. The overflow flag can be cleared using the CLV command.

Chapter 9 SUMMARY

1. The microprocessor contains a special purpose register, the processor status code register.

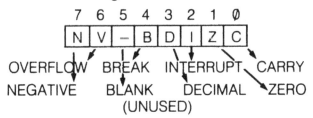

2. CARRY — SEC, CLC

    BCS, BCC

    Set if carry condition occurs.

3. ZERO — BEQ, BNE
   Set if a result or transfer = 0.

4. BRK is an instruction which sets the break flag and halts the microprocessor (useful for debugging purposes).

5. INTERRUPT — SEI, CLI

   See Chapters 11, 12.

6. DECIMAL — SED, CLD

   Sets decimal mode. Addition and subtraction are done using BCD (Binary Coded Decimal).

7. Two's complement numbering represents numbers from -128 to 127.

   negative $X = (\text{complement } (X)) + 1$

8. NEGATIVE — flag set if bit 7 of result is turned on ($=1$)

   BMI, BPL

9. OVERFLOW — set on two's complement carry

   CLV

   BVS, BVC

Chapter 10
Logical Operators and Bit Manipulators

Changing bits within memory

In this chapter we will be looking at a group of instructions unlike any others we have looked at previously, yet they are absolutely fundamental to the workings of a computer. They are the 'logical' or 'Boolean' operations. They are the commands AND (Logical AND), ORA (Logical OR), and EOR (Logical Exclusive OR). These functions can be built up using fairly simple circuitry, and almost all functions of the computer are built up by series of these circuits. The logical operations of these circuits are available to us through these instructions and it is this, and not the hardware, with which we will concern ourselves in this chapter.

We know that bytes of memory and the registers are made up of groups of eight bits:

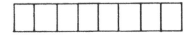

To explain the functions of these instructions, we look at their operation on one bit and then assume that this operation is done on all eight bits at once. A logical operator is like a mathematical function in that it takes in two pieces of data and puts out its result as one, e.g.

$$4 + 5 = 9$$

In this case however the data coming in is going to be single bit values, either 1's or 0's. To define a logical function we draw up a 'truth' table showing all possible inputs and the associated output.

INPUT 1 / INPUT 2	Ø	1
Ø	OUTPUT FOR Ø, Ø	OUTPUT FOR Ø, 1
1	OUTPUT FOR 1, Ø	OUTPUT FOR 1, 1

The logical AND

The first instruction we will deal with is the AND instruction. This performs a logical AND of the accumulator and the specified memory, leaving the result in A. The result of a logical AND is 1 if input is a 1 **and** input 2 is a 1. The truth table for this function looks like:

AND

MEMORY / ACCUMULATOR	Ø	1
Ø	Ø	Ø
1	Ø	1

When extended to an eight bit byte this means that:

```
        Ø 1 1 Ø 1 Ø 1 1
AND     1 Ø 1 1 1 Ø 1 Ø
   =    Ø Ø 1 Ø 1 Ø 1 Ø
```

The zero flag is set if the result = Ø, i.e. if there are no coincident ones in the bits of the two bytes used.

The AND instruction is useful in creating a 'mask' to turn off certain bits within a byte. Suppose, within a byte of any value, we wish to turn off the 3rd, 5th and 6th bits. We would create a 'mask' with only the 3rd, 5th and 6th bits turned **off** and AND this with the byte in question.

```
              7 6 5 4 3 2 1 Ø
Mask =        1 Ø Ø 1 Ø 1 1 1     = $97
AND   #$97
```

would turn off the 3rd, 5th and 6th bits of whatever was in the accumulator.

78

The logical OR

The second instruction we will look at is the ORA instruction. This does a logical OR of the accumulator with the specified memory leaving the result in the accumulator.

The OR function outputs a 1 if input 1 is a 1 **or** input 2 is a 1. The truth table for this function looks like:

OR	MEMORY / ACCUMULATOR	$\emptyset$	1
	$\emptyset$	$\emptyset$	1
	1	1	1

When extended to an eight bit byte this means that:

		$\emptyset$	1	$\emptyset$	1	$\emptyset$	$\emptyset$	1	$\emptyset$
ORA		$\emptyset$	$\emptyset$	1	1	1	$\emptyset$	1	$\emptyset$
=		$\emptyset$	1	1	1	1	$\emptyset$	1	$\emptyset$

The zero flag is set if both bytes are used and hence the result is zero.

The ORA instruction is useful for turning on certain bits within a byte using the masking technique.

Suppose we want to turn on the 2nd, 3rd and 7th bits within a byte. We would use a mask with only the 2nd, 3rd and 7th bits turned **on**.

```
              7 6 5 4 3 2 1 0
Mask  =      1 0 0 0 1 1 0 0    =  $8C
ORA  #$8C
```

would turn on the 2nd, 3rd and 7th bits of whatever was in the accumulator.

The logical exclusive OR

The last of the logical operators is the EOR. This does a logical exclusive — OR of the accumulator and memory leaving the result in A. The exclusive — OR function outputs a 1 if input is a 1 **or** input 2 is a 1 **but** not if both are a 1. The truth table for this function looks like:

EOR	MEMORY / ACCUMULATOR	$\emptyset$	1
	$\emptyset$	$\emptyset$	1
	1	1	$\emptyset$

79

When extended to an eight bit byte the exclusive — OR produces:

$$\begin{array}{c}\boxed{1\,|\,0\,|\,1\,|\,1\,|\,1\,|\,0\,|\,0\,|\,1}\\[2pt]\text{EOR}\ \boxed{1\,|\,0\,|\,1\,|\,0\,|\,0\,|\,1\,|\,0\,|\,1}\\[2pt]=\ \boxed{0\,|\,0\,|\,0\,|\,1\,|\,1\,|\,1\,|\,0\,|\,0}\end{array}$$

The exclusive — OR is used to complement (invert) certain bits within a byte using masking.

To invert the 1st, 2nd and 4th bits of a byte we would use a mask with those bits turned **on**.

$$\begin{array}{c}7\ 6\ 5\ 4\ 3\ 2\ 1\ 0\\[2pt]\text{Mask} = \boxed{0\,|\,0\,|\,0\,|\,1\,|\,0\,|\,1\,|\,1\,|\,0} = \$16\\[2pt]\text{EOR }\#\$16\end{array}$$

would invert those bits of the accumulator.

Type the following program into ALPA to test these instructions:

```
NEW
10 A9CA          LDA #$CA
20 299F          AND #$9F
30 8D3403        STA $0334
40 A9A2          LDA #$A2
50 0984          ORA #$84
60 4D3403        EOR $0334
70 8D3403        STA $0334
80 60            RTS
WATCH    (address? 334)
```

Program summary

Line 10		A = $CA	11001010
Line 20 AND $9F		A = $8A	10001010
Line 30	STORE	A = $334	10001010
Line 40		A = $A2	10100010
Line 50 ORA $84		A = #A6	10100110
Line 60 EOR $334		A = $2C	00101100

ENTER and RUN this program

and verify the results with those we have reached.

The bit instruction

There is a useful instruction in the 6510 instruction set which does an interesting set of tests and comparisons. We discussed in Chapter 6 how the CMP command did a subtraction setting the status flags but not storing the result. Similarly BIT (compare memory bits with the accumulator) does a logical AND of A and memory, setting only the Z flag as a result. The bit instruction also copies bit 7 into the negative flag and bit 6 into the overflow flag.

Rotating bits within a byte

We will now discuss four other bit manipulation instructions and some of their consequences. The first instruction we will look at is ASL (Arithmetic Shift Left). This instruction shifts all the bits in the specified byte left by one bit, introducing a zero at the low end and moving the high bit off into the carry flag.

CARRY   7 6 5 4 3 2 1 0

hence

C = ? | 0 | 1 | 0 | 1 | 0 | 1 | 0 | 1 |

becomes

C = 0 | 1 | 0 | 1 | 0 | 1 | 0 | 1 | 0 |

and

C = ? | 1 | 0 | 1 | 1 | 0 | 1 | 1 | 0 |

becomes

C = 1 | 0 | 1 | 1 | 0 | 1 | 1 | 0 | 0 |

Back in Chapter 3 when we explained hex and binary we mentioned that each bit had the value of 2 $_{position - 1}$

i.e. | 128 | 64 | 32 | 16 | 8 | 4 | 2 | 1 |

You will notice that the value of each box is two times the value of the box to the right of it, hence:

00000001 x 2 = 00000010   and
00001000 x 2 = 00010000

and furthermore

00111001 x 2 = 01110010

The operation required to multiply any byte by two is the operation performed by the ASL instruction.

To use our examples from before:

C = ?   01010101 ($55)×2 → C = 0   10101010 ($AA)

and

C = ?   10110110 ($B6)×2 → C = 1   01101100 ($6C + CARRY)

Type in the following program:

```
NEW
10 A90A              LDA #$0A
20 0A                ASL A
30 8D3403            STA $0334
40 60                RTS
WATCH       (address? 334)
ENTER and RUN
```

Line 20 uses the 'accumulator' addressing mode. It uses the contents of the accumulator as data and returns the result there.

NOTE: this is different to implied addressing because ASL may be used on data from memory.

We can use this instruction to multiply a number by any power of 2 (1, 2, 4, 8. . .). To use the previous program to multiply by eight instead of two, insert the following two lines:

```
15 0A                ASL A
25 0A                ASL A
```
ENTER and RUN the program with these alterations:
$0A x 8 = 50

Rotation with carry

As with our addition routines, we may find we want to multiply numbers greater than 255 (two or more byte numbers). To do this there is a shift command which uses the carry on the input end of the shift as well as the output end:

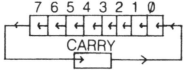

The instruction to do this is ROL (Rotate One bit Left). To do a two byte multiply by four, type the following lines:

```
 5 A917              LDA #$17
 6 8D3503            STA $0335
18 2E3503            ROL $0335
25 2E3503            ROL $0335
LIST
```

We are multiplying the two byte number $170A by four.

NOTE: 1. To avoid swapping registers we have used ROL absolute which stores its result back in memory.

2. We have rotated both bytes once and then rotated both again. Rotating the low byte twice and then the high byte twice

would not work, because the high bit from the low byte would be lost when the carry was used in the second ASL.

ENTER and RUN
type WATCH   (Address ? 335)
RUN the program again

Put together the high and low bytes of the answer and check that it equals four times our original number.

Rotating to the right

LSR and ROR are the equivalent instructions to ASL and ROL, except that they shift the bits in the opposite direction.

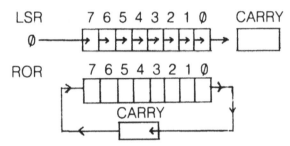

Just as their opposites can be thought of as multiplications by two, so these can be thought of as division by two, and can be similarly extended to multi-byte arithmetic. After division, the number left in the byte is the integer part of the result and the bits which have been shifted out represent the remainder, e.g.

$1D ÷ $08   =   3   remainder 5

```
        00011101    = 29        remainder
LSR ÷ 2
        00001110    = 14        →  1 = 1
LSR ÷ 4
        00000111    = 7         → 01 = 1
LSR ÷ 8
        00000011    = 3         → 101 = 5
```

NOTE: Just because the shift and rotate instructions can be used for arithmetic, do not forget their use for shifting bits, e.g. shifting into carry for testing.

Clever multiplication

We have said that by shifting bits we can multiply by any power of 2 (1, 2, 4, 8 . . ., 128). These are the same values that represent each bit within a byte. We have shown in Chapter 3 that by adding these values we can produce any number between 0 and 255.

If we then multiply by each of these values and add the results, this process is equivalent to multiplying by any value from 0 to 255, e.g.

$$
\begin{aligned}
\$16 \times \$59 &= 00010110 \times \$59 \\
&= 00010000 \times \$59 \\
&+ 00000100 \times \$59 \\
&+ 00000010 \times \$59 \\
&= 16 \times \$59 + 4 \times \$59 + 2 \times \$59
\end{aligned}
$$

which we know how to work out from our previous multiplication.

This is the algorithm we will use in our generalised multiplication routine. We will rotate (multiply by two) one number, and add it to the total, for each bit turned on in the other byte, e.g.

```
10110 x $59
rotate   $59                              1  0  1  1 [0]
rotate   $59       add to total           1  0  1 [1] 0
rotate   $59       add to total           1  0 [1] 1  0
rotate   $59                              1 [0] 1  1  0
rotate   $59       add to total          [1] 0  1  1  0
```

For simplicity's sake, our generalised multiplication routine will only handle results less than 255.

To multiply $1B by $09 type:

```
NEW
10  A91B          LDA #$1B
20  8D3403        STA $0334
30  A909          LDA #$09
40  8D3503        STA $0335
50  A900          LDA #$00
60  6E3503        ROR $0335
70  2E3503        ROL $0335
80  4E3403        LSR $0334
90  90L120        BCC L120
100 18            CLC
110 6D3503        ADC $0335
120 D0L70         BNE L70
130 8D3603        STA $0336
140 60            RTS
```

Program summary

lines 10 - 60   initialise values to be multiplied and the total to 0. The ROR followed by ROL has no effect the first time through but only the ROL is within the loop.

line 70   except for the first time through, this multiplies one of the numbers (2) by two each time around the loop.

lines 80 - 90	rotates the other number (1) bit by bit into the carry, and then tests the carry to see if the other number (2) should be added this time around the loop. If the carry is clear, the possibility that the number (1) has been shifted completely through ($= \emptyset$ — Multiplication is completed) is tested — line 120.
lines 100 - 110	add to the total (in A) the number (2) which is being multiplied by two each time around the loop.
line 120	if the branch on line 90 was taken, this will test for the end of multiplication (number (1) $= \emptyset$ shifted completely through). If the branch on line 90 was not taken, this branch on not equal will always be true because we are adding a number (2) greater than zero to a total which will not be greater than 255.
lines 130 - 140	END.

NOTE: this multiplication routine is much more efficient than the one given in Chapter 7. By that method we would have had to loop at least nine times, whereas with this, had we swapped and used 9 as number (1) and $1B as number (2), we would have only looped four times (number of bits needed to make 9 — 1001).

Type:

```
WATCH        (address ? 336)
ENTER
RUN
```

and verify the results.

Now change the numbers used to perform a different calculation (make sure the answer <256), e.g.

```
10  A906           LDA #$06
30  A925           LDA #$25
ENTER and RUN
```

with these values and again verify the results for yourself.

Chapter 10   SUMMARY

1. AND

	0	1
0	0	0
1	0	1

most often used to mask **off** bits.

2. ORA

	0	1
0	0	1
1	1	1

most often used to mask **on** bits.

3. EOR (exclusive or)

	Ø	1
Ø	Ø	1
1	1	Ø

most often used to mask **invert** bits.

4. BIT   performs AND without storing the result.

Z is set or cleared
N becomes bit 7
V becomes bit 6

5. ASL   7 6 5 4 3 2 1 Ø   Arithmetic Shift Left

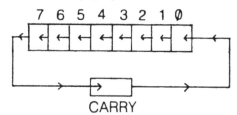

CARRY

most often used to multiply by 2.

6. ROL   7 6 5 4 3 2 1 Ø   Rotate One Bit Left

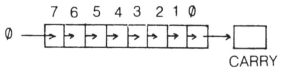

CARRY

7. LSR   Logical Shift Right

7 6 5 4 3 2 1 Ø

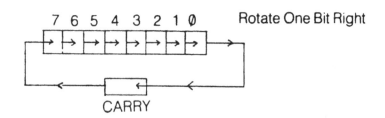

CARRY

8. ROR   7 6 5 4 3 2 1 Ø   Rotate One Bit Right

CARRY

Chapter 11
Details of Program Control

The program counter

We have talked a lot about the different operations that the microprocessor can perform, but we have said very little about how it goes about those tasks. This is perfectly alright, because in most cases we don't need to know. In one case, however, knowing how the microprocessor is operating leads us into a whole new list of commands and a powerful area of the microprocessor's capabilities.

The microprocessor contains a special purpose, two byte register called the Program Counter (PC), whose sole job is to keep track of where the next instruction is coming from in memory. In other words, the program counter contains the address of the next byte to be loaded into the microprocessor and used as a command.

If we think of our post office boxes again, each holding either an instruction (opcode) or the data/address it acts upon (operand), this is what our program looks like, e.g.

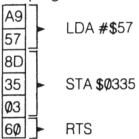

To 'run' our post office box program, we would go through each box in turn and act on the data within each box. Now imagine there was a large clock type counter showing a box address which we looked at to know which box to find. Normally this counter would go up one by one, taking the next byte in order. However, if it wanted us to move to a new area of the boxes, it would just flash up the address of the next instruction it wanted us to find. This is exactly how the JMP command operates.

Storing into the program counter

The instruction JMP $address only loads the two byte $address into the program counter, the next instruction is then loaded from memory at that address, and a JMP has been executed.

87

NOTE: the branch instructions add or subtract from the program counter in a similar way, thereby creating a 'relative' jump.

The program counter and subroutines

If it were possible to store the program counter just before doing a JMP and changing it to a new address, we would later be able to return to the same place in memory by reloading that stored piece of memory back into the program counter. In other words, if we had noticed that the post office box counter was about to change, and we noted down the address it showed (our current address) before it changed, we would at some future stage place that back on the counter and return to where we had left off.

This, of course, is a subroutine structure, e.g.

```
10 PRINT "HELLO WORLD"
20 GOSUB 100
30 PRINT "I'M FINE"
40 END
100 PRINT "HOW ARE YOU?"
110 RETURN
```

would print:

```
HELLO WORLD
HOW ARE YOU?
I'M FINE
```

We said at the beginning of the book that a machine language program can be thought of as a subroutine called from BASIC using the SYS command.

You can also create subroutines from within a machine language program. They are called using the JSR (Jump to Subroutine) command. As when called from BASIC, to return from a machine language subroutine you use the RTS (Return From Subroutine) command.

Type the following program:

```
NEW
N WATCH
 10 A901        LDA #$01
 20 8D15D0      STA $D015
 30 8DF807      STA $07F8
 40 A932        LDA #$32
 50 8D00D0      STA $D000
 60 8D01D0      STA $D001
 70 20L110      JSR L110
 80 C9FA        CMP #$FA
 90 D0L70       BNE L70
100 60          RTS
```

88

```
110 EE01D0        INC $D001  ┐
120 AD00D0        LDA $D000  │
130 18            CLC        ├─subroutine
140 6904          ADC #$04   │
150 8D00D0        STA $D000  ┘
160 60            RTS
ENTER
RUN
```

Remember that these programs go extremely fast. If it looks like your sprite does not move, RUN the program several times. You may catch a brief glimpse of it moving across the screen.

It is good programming style to use subroutines for two major reasons. Firstly, it is easy to locate and fix errors within subroutines. They can be tested and fixed independently of the rest of the program. Secondly, by using subroutines it is possible to build up a 'library' of useful subroutines, e.g. sprite movers, screen clearers, byte finders etc. which may be added as a subroutine to any program.

We have said that the return address of the subroutine is stored away but we have not said anything about **how** it is stored. We want some sort of filing system to store this address which will give us a number of necessary features.

The stack control structure

Firstly, it must be flexible and easy to use. Secondly, we would like to be able to provide for the possibility that a subroutine will be called from within a subroutine (called from within a subroutine, called from within . . .). In this case we have to use a system which will not only remember a return address for each of the subroutines called, but will have to remember which is the correct return address for each subroutine. The system which we use to store the addresses on a data structure is called a 'stack'. A stack is a LIFO structure (Last In First Out). When an RTS is reached, we want the last address put on the stack to be used as a return address for the subroutine.

Imagine the stack to be one of those spikes that people sometimes keep messages on.

Every time you see a JSR instruction, you copied down the return address onto a scrap of paper from the post office box counter. As soon as you had done this, you spiked the piece of paper on the stack. If you came across another JSR you merely repeated the process. Now when you come across an RTS, the only piece of paper you can take off the spike (stack) is the top one. The others are all blocked by those on top of them. This top piece of paper will always contain the correct return address for the subroutine you are returning from (that which was most recently called).

89

Subroutines and the stack

The JSR and RTS commands do this automatically using the system stack. The stack sits in memory from $100 to $1FF (Page 1) and grows downwards. (Imagine the spike turned upside down). This makes no difference to its operation. The top of the stack (or actually the bottom) is marked by a special purpose register within the microprocessor called the Stack Pointer (SP). When a JSR is done, the two byte program counter is put on the stack and the stack pointer (SP) is decremented by two (a two byte address is put on).

BEFORE

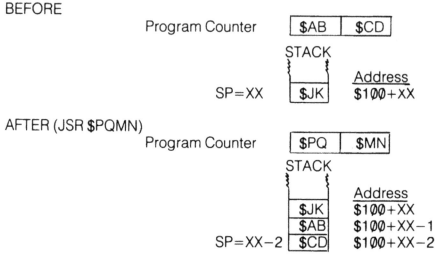

An RTS takes the top two bytes off the stack and returns them to the program counter. The stack pointer is incremented by two.

BEFORE

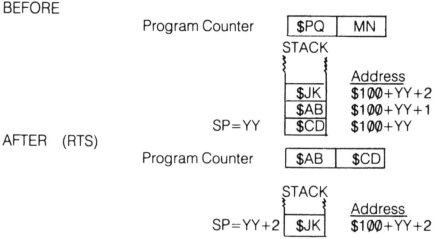

DUMP memory from $100 to $200 to have a look at the stack memory.

Insert the following lines into the program to call a subroutine from within the subroutine.

90

```
125 20L170        JSR L170
170 C950          CMP #$50
180 90L195        BCC L195
190 EE 01D0       INC #D001
195 60            RTS
```
ENTER and RUN the program.

One major advantage of the stack is that it can also be used to store data by using the instructions PHA (Push Accumulator onto the Stack) and PLA (Pull Accumulator off the Stack) respectively to put the contents of the accumulator on and off the stack.

WARNING: make sure you put things on and off the stack in the correct order.

If you use the RTS while there is extra data on the top of the stack, the RTS will return to an address made up of the two top bytes of the stack whatever they are.

Let us use these instructions to test the operation of the stack. Type:

```
NEW
WATCH            (address ? 334)
  10 20L40       JSR L40
  20 EE 20D0     INC $D020
  30 60          RTS
  40 68          PLA
  50 AA          TAX
  60 68          PLA
  70 8E3403      STX $0334
  80 8D3503      STA $0335
  90 48          PHA
 100 8A          TXA
 110 48          PHA
 120 60          RTS
```

Program summary

Line 10	JSR — return address (address of next instruction is placed on the stack). (Actually it points to the byte **before** the next instruction because the PC is incremented each time before a byte is 'fetched' from memory.)
Line 20	increments screen border colour (see Appendix 6) just to show that the program has returned satisfactorily. satisfactorily.
Line 30	END
Lines 40 - 60	take the top two bytes of the stack.
Lines 70 - 80	store them low byte/high byte at $334, $335.
Lines 90 - 110	return bytes to stack IN CORRECT ORDER
Line 120	END of Subroutine.

ENTER and RUN this program. Change watch to test address $335, RUN again. Put the results together and compare them against the expected address.

The two instructions TSX (Transfer SP into X) and TXS (Transfer X into SP) are available to do direct manipulations on the SP. Write a program with a subroutine within a subroutine, both of which save the SP in memory (via X) to see the change in SP when a subroutine is called and when an RTS is executed.

The stack and interrupts

We mentioned in Chapter 9 the BRK command and its use in debugging programs by halting them and giving you a chance to examine variables in 'mid-flight'. What the BRK command actually does is something like the operation of a JSR. The BRK command executes a JSR indirect on $FFFE, $FFFF. In other words, the contents of those bytes are put into the PC and the program continues there (at a ROM break handling routine). The BRK command also pushes the value of the processor status code register (P) onto the stack.

This can be done outside the BRK command using the PHP (Push Processor Status byte) and PLP (Pull Processor Status byte) instructions. This all leads up to a fairly major area of machine language programming on the Commodore 64 — Interrupts. However, we will not cover these, as they are too advanced for this book but we will attempt to tell you how, where and why they work. In general, an interrupt is sent to the microprocessor by the computer's hardware to alert it to something going on in the outside world which requires its attention, e.g. a key being pressed, real time clock, or graphics alerts (see Chapter 12, Appendix 8 and Appendix 6 respectively).

These interrupts are hardware signals and their effect is to halt the microprocessor in the middle of whatever it was doing, and jump to an interrupt service routine (via vectors at $FFFE, $FFFF).

In a similar way to the BRK, an interrupt stores the PC on the stack (with the address of the instruction it was in the middle of doing — **not** the next instruction). It then stores the status register (P) on the stack and does an indirect jump on the contents of location $FFFE and $FFFF, which take it to a ROM interrupt routine.

You can control the interrupt service routines to handle interrupts from clock timers or other sources in your own way to do things such as move objects at a constant predetermined speed and increment time of day clocks, as well as many other uses. Some of the methods for doing this are described in the next chapter.

Press RUNSTOP-RESTORE to return the screen to normal. Type GOTO 2020.

Chapter 11 SUMMARY

1. Program Counter (PC) points to the next byte in memory to be used as an instruction.

2. JMP stores address in PC.

3. Branches add or subtract from PC.

4. JSR stores PC on stack and stores new address in PC (subroutine).

5. RTS takes the top two bytes off stack stores in PC (return address).

6. The stack can only have things put on at one end. They can only be taken off from the same end in the same order they were put on.

7. The stack pointer keeps track of the 'top' of the stack.

   RTS ⇒ SP=SP+2
   JSR ⇒ SP=SP−2

8. PHA, PLA store and retrieve the accumulator from the stack. Be sure to take things off the stack in the same order they went on.

9. TXS, TSX transfer contents between the stack pointer and X.

10. BRK   PC   →Stack (2 bytes)
                Status byte   →Stack
                Contents of
                (FFFE,FFFF)   →PC

11. PHP, PLP push and pull a processor status word onto the stack.

12. Interrupts come from chips external to the microprocessor
                   PC   →Stack (2 bytes)
                Status byte   →Stack
                (FFFE,FFFF)   →PC

    They are handled by ROM handling routines.

93

Chapter 12
Dealing with the Operating System

The Kernal

This chapter will tell you something about dealing with the operating system of the Commodore 64. The operating system is a program in ROM sometimes called the Kernal. It sits in memory from $E000 to $FFFF and deals with the hardware side of the computer (other ROM deals with BASIC or Characters etc). There are routines in the kernal for opening and closing files, printing characters to the screen, getting characters from the keyboard, moving the cursor around the screen, loading and saving files, and other such mundane but necessary tasks.

In this chapter we will give examples of how to use a few of these routines (the Appendices will give clues to more but the rest is up to you). Armed with these methods and the information given in the Appendices (and any you can scrounge from elsewhere), you will be able to create programs which can easily and effectively communicate with the outside world. One of the major uses of the kernal is in dealing with interrupts. Interrupts may be sent by peripherals, the sound chip and the clock as well as many other places. The clock sends out an interrupt every 1/50 of a second (1/60 in the U.S.A.). This interrupt is used by the kernal to update the time of day clock and to check the keyboard for a keypress.

We said in the previous chapter that an interrupt, as well as putting a return address and the status byte on the stack, did an indirect JUMP on the contents of memory locations $FFFE and $FFFF. We said this was directed to the operating systems interrupt handler in ROM. This ROM routine does its work and then gives the programmer access to the interrupt process by doing a jump through interrupt vectors placed in RAM at locations $314, $315 (low byte/high byte format). Since these vectors are placed in RAM they can be changed to point to our program.

Our interrupt routine must do one of two things. It must either return via the operating system when it is finished (via the address which was in the interrupt vector before we changed it) or we must 'clean up' the system and return properly from an interrupt. In practice it is generally easier to take the first choice. If we do it on our own, our program must finish by:

1. Taking the registers off the stack. When the ROM interrupt routine is called it saves all the registers on the stack. These must be returned to the registers in the same order.
2. We must re-enable interrupts. The ROM routine, as well as doing an SEI which sets the interrupt flag in the status register, turns off the interrupts from their source.
3. Do an RTI (Return From Interrupt).

Have a look at the ROM interrupt exit routine by disassembling memory from $EA31 onwards.

NOTE: SEI (Set Interrupt Flag) will stop the microprocessor from receiving any more interrupts. This is set at the beginning of the interrupt routine to make sure that any time-critical interrupts are completed before another is started (to allow for the chance of being interrupted during the interrupt routine).

CLI (Clear Interrupt Flag)

This re-enables interrupts to occur. This instruction is used at the end of some interrupt routines, or if the interrupt is not time-critical.

RTI (Return From Interrupt)

Somewhat like the RTS, this instruction removes those things placed on the stack by the interrupts (status byte, program counter), thereby returning to where the program left off (with the status byte undisturbed). This, by restoring the status byte, will clear the interrupt flag (it could not have been set when the interrupt was received!)

Our sample interrupt program which follows is in two parts. The first part sets up the interrupt vectors at location $314, $315; it is called once when the program is RUN and then returns. The second part, which is pointed to by the altered interrupt vectors, is called 50 times a second (when an interrupt is made by the clock chip).

Type the following:

```
NWATCH
NEW
10 A94C          LDA #$4C
12 8DF0CF        STA $CFF0
14 A949          LDA #$49
16 8DF1CF        STA $CFF1
18 A953          LDA #$53
20 8DF2CF        STA $CCF 2
22 A954          LDA #$54
```

```
24 8DF3CF              STA $CFF3
26 A90D                LDA #$0D
28 8DF4CF              STA $CFF4
30 A900                LDA #$00
32 8DF5CF              STA $CFF5
34 78                  SEI
36 A92B                LDA #$2B
38 8D1403              STA $0314
40 A9C0                LDA #$C0
42 8D1503              STA $0315
44 58                  CLI
46 60                  RTS

60 209FFF              JSR $FF9F
62 A6C6                LDX $C6
64 F0L90               BEQ L90
66 CA                  DEX
68 BD7702              LDA $0277,X
70 C985                CMP #$85
72 D0L90               BNE L90
74 A0FF                LDY #$FF
78 C8                  INY
80 E8                  INX
82 B9F0CF              LDA $CFF0,Y
84 9D7702              STA $0277,X
86 D0L78               BNE L78
88 86C6                STX $C6
90 4C31EA              JMP $EA31
```

Program summary

This program sets up the function key F1 to print LIST RETURN when the key is hit. This can be done for any string for any key and can save you from typing commonly used commands.

Part 1	lines 10-46	initialisation
	lines 10-32	set up in memory, from $CFF0 onwards, a string of characters, L-I-S-T RETURN followed by a zero signifying the end of the string.
	line 34	turns off the interrupts by setting the interrupt flag. This **must** be done while changing the interrupt vectors.
	lines 36-42	change the interrupt vectors to point to Part 2 of the program. (Part 2 will start from location $C02B — count the bytes.)
	lines 44-46	re-enable the interrupts and END.

Part 2	lines 60-90	will be put at $C02B and be called 50 times a second via the interrupt vectors.
	line 60	JSR to the kernal's keyboard scan routine. This routine scans the keyboard and returns with any key pressed in the input buffer at $277 onwards.
	line 62	loads X with the length of the input buffer (pointer to next empty space in buffer).
	line 64	if buffer empty return.
	line 66	points pointer to previous entry in buffer.
	lines 68-72	load previous character if it is not the F1 key return.
	lines 74-86	put string ('LIST RETURN') into buffer.
	line 88	saves new pointer to buffer length.
	line 90	returns via ROM interrupt handler.

Type ENTER and RUN.

The program should return without output. Press the F1 function key. It has automatically typed the LIST command for you and displayed the program.

The tables presented in the Appendices are not intended to explain every (or even some) ROM kernal routine in detail. That would provide enough text for an entire book on its own. This book does give you the entry points (addresses) of **some** of the kernal routines, and gives you details on the requirements and actions of a few of the most commonly used routines. The only way to find out more is by a combination of trial and error and by disassembling the routines as they are in memory.

GOOD LUCK!

OH! There is one 6510 instruction which I have not yet mentioned. That is the NOP (No Operation) instruction. Although it does nothing, it takes a certain amount of time to do. It is used surprisingly often within a time delay loop, or to fill a patch within a program where you have decided to remove instructions. The value for for the instruction NOP is $EA.

Chapter 12 SUMMARY

1. Kernal in ROM handles the computer's contact with the outside world.

2. Kernal resides in memory from $E000 to $FFFF.

3. SEI — Sets interrupt flag and excludes any further interrupts from occurring.

4. CLI — clears interrupt flag, re-enables interrupts.
5. RTI — return from interrupt.
   STACK→Status byte
   STACK→PC (2 bytes)
6. NOP — no operation.

APPENDICES

Introduction to the Appendices

We have provided you with charts and tables of useful information necessary for machine code programming on the Commodore 64. The information presented will stand as a useful reference long after you have left 'beginner' status but until then these tables can be used by the beginner. We have provided explanations and occasionally examples of the most useful parts of the tables. Those that have no accompanying explanation are really beyond the scope of this book and are included for interest's sake, as well as to give you a handy reference and a start towards more complex and intricate programming in the future.

Appendix 1

6510 Instruction Codes

These tables should be a constant reference while writing machine code or assembly code programs. There is a list of every instruction with a description, available addressing modes, instruction format, number of bytes used, the hex code for the instruction, and a list of the status flags changed as a result of the instruction.

6510 Microprocessor Instructions in alphabetical order

ADC	Add Memory to Accumulator with Carry	LDA	Load Accumulator with Memory
AND	"AND" Memory with Accumulator	LDX	Load Index X with Memory
ASL	Shift Left One Bit (Memory or Accumulator)	LDY	Load Index Y with Memory
BCC	Branch on Carry Clear	LSR	Shift Right one Bit (Memory or Accumulator)
BCS	Branch on Carry Set	NOP	No Operation
BEQ	Branch on Result Zero	ORA	"OR" Memory with Accumulator
BIT	Test Bits in Memory with Accumulator	PHA	Push Accumulator on Stack
		PHP	Push Processor Status on Stack
BMI	Branch on Result Minus	PLA	Pull Accumulator from Stack
BNE	Branch on Result not Zero	PLP	Pull Processor Status from Stack
BPL	Branch on Result Plus	ROL	Rotate One Bit Left (Memory or Accumulator)
BRK	Force Break		
BVC	Branch on Overflow Clear	ROR	Rotate One Bit Right (Memory or Accumulator)
BVS	Branch on Overflow Set		
CLC	Clear Carry Flag	RTI	Return from Interrupt
CLD	Clear Decimal Mode	RTS	Return from Subroutine
CLI	Clear Interrupt Disable Bit	SBC	Subtract Memory from Accumulator with Borrow
CLV	Clear Overflow flag		
CMP	Compare Memory and Accumulator	SEC	Set Carry Flag
		SED	Set Decimal Mode
CPX	Compare Memory and Index X	SEI	Set Interrupt Disable Status
CPY	Compare Memory and Index Y	STA	Store Accumulator in Memory
DEC	Decrement Memory by One	STX	Store Index X in Memory
DEX	Decrement Index X by One	STY	Store Index Y in Memory
DEY	Decrement Index Y by One	TAX	Transfer Accumulator to Index X
EOR	"Exclusive-Or" Memory with Accumulator	TAY	Transfer Accumulator to Index Y
		TSX	Transfer Stack Pointer to Index X
INC	Increment Memory by One	TXA	Transfer Index X to Accumulator
INX	Increment Index X by One	TXS	Transfer Index X to Stack Pointer
INY	Increment Index Y by One	TYA	Transfer Index Y to Accumulator
JMP	Jump to New Location		
JSR	Jump to New Location Saving Return Address		

6510 Instruction Codes

Name Description	Addressing Mode	Assembly Language Form	No Bytes	HEX OP Code	Status Register
ADC Add memory to accumulator with carry	Immediate Zero Page Zero Page.X Absolute Absolute.X Absolute.Y (Indirect.X) (Indirect).Y	ADC #Oper ADC Oper ADC Oper.X ADC Oper ADC Oper.X ADC Oper.Y AND (Oper.X) ADC (Oper).Y	2 2 2 3 3 3 2 2	69 65 75 6D 7D 79 61 71	N V - B D I Z C • • • •
AND "AND" memory with accumulator	Immediate Zero Page Zero Page.X Absolute Absolute.X Absolute.Y (Indirect.X) (Indirect).Y	AND #Oper AND Oper AND Oper.X AND Oper AND Oper.X AND Oper.Y AND (Oper.X) AND (Oper.)Y	2 2 2 3 3 3 2 2	29 25 35 2D 3D 39 31 31	N V - B D I Z C • •
ASL Shift left one bit (Memory or Accumulator)	Accumulator Zero Page Zero Page.X Absolute Absolute.X	ASL A ASL Oper ASL Oper.X ASL Oper ASL Oper X	1 2 2 3 3	0A 06 16 0E 1E	N V - B D I Z C • • •

C←[7 6 5 4 3 2 1 0]←[0]

Name Description	Addressing Mode	Assembly Language Form	No Bytes	HEX OP Code	Status Register
BBC Branch on carry clear	Relative	BBC Oper	2	90	N V - B D I Z C
BCS Branch on carry set	Relative	BCS Oper	2	B0	N V - B D I Z C
BEQ Branch on result zero	Relative	BEQ Oper	2	F0	N V - B D I Z C
BIT Test bits in memory with accumulator	Zero Page Absolute	BIT Oper BIT Oper	1 3	24 2C	N V - B D I Z C M M • 7 6
BMI Branch on result minus	Relative	BMI Oper	2	30	N V - B D I Z C
BNE Branch on result not zero	Relative	BNE Oper	2	D0	N V - B D I Z C
BPL Branch on result plus	Relative	BPL oper	2	10	N V - B D I Z C
BRK Force Break	Implied	BRK	1	00	N V - B D I Z C 1 1
BVC Branch on overflow clear	Relative	BVC Oper	2	50	N V - B D I Z C

6510 Instruction Codes

Name Description	Addressing Mode	Assembly Language Form	No Bytes	HEX OP Code	Status Register
BVS Branch on overflow set	Relative	BVS Oper	2	70	N V - B D I Z C
CLC Clear carry flag	Implied	CLC	1	18	N V - B D I Z C 0
CLD Clear decimal mode	Implied	CLD	1	D8	N V - B D I Z C 0
CLI Clear interrupt flag	Implied	CLI	1	58	N V - B D I Z C 0
CLV Clear overflow flag	Implied	CLV	1	B8	N V - B D I Z C 0
CMP Compare memory and accumulator	Immediate	CMP #Oper	2	C9	N V - B D I Z C • • •
	Zero Page	CMP Oper	2	C5	
	Zero Page.X	CMP Oper.X	2	D5	
	Absolute	CMP Oper	3	CD	
	Absolute.X	CMP Oper.X	3	DD	
	Absolute.Y	CMP Oper.Y	3	D9	
	(Indirect.X)	CMP (Oper.X)	2	C1	
	(Indirect).Y	CMP (Oper).Y	2	D1	
CPX Compare memory and index X	Immediate	CPX #Oper	2	E0	N V - B D I Z C • • •
	Zero Page	CPX Oper	2	E4	
	Absolute	CPX Oper	3	EC	
CPY Compare memory and index Y	Immediate	CPY #Oper	2	C0	N V - B D I Z C • • •
	Zero Page	CPY Oper	2	C4	
	Absolute	CPY Oper	3	CC	
DEC Decrement memory by one	Zero Page	DEC Oper	2	C6	N V - B D I Z C • •
	Zero Page.X	DEC Oper.X	2	D6	
	Absolute	DEC Oper	3	CE	
	Absolute.X	DEC Oper.X	3	DE	
DEX Decrement index X by one	Implied	DEX	1	DA	N V - B D I Z C • •
DEY Decrement index Y by one	Implied	DEY	1	88	N V - B D I Z C • •

6510 Instruction Codes

Name Description	Addressing Mode	Assembly Language Form	No Bytes	HEX OP Code	Status Register
EOR					N V - B D I Z C
"Exclusive Or" memory	Immediate	EOR #Oper	2	49	• •
with accumulator	Zero Page	EOR Oper	2	45	
	Zero Page X	EOR Oper.X	2	55	
	Absolute	EOR Oper	3	4D	
	Absolute.X	EOR Oper.X	3	5D	
	Absolute.Y	EOR Oper.Y	3	59	
	(Indirect.X)	EOR (Oper.X)	2	41	
	(Indirect).Y	EOR (Oper).Y	2	51	
INC					N V - B D I Z C
Increment memory	Zero Page	INC. Oper	2	E6	• •
by one	Zero Page.X	INC Oper.X	2	F6	
	Absolute	INC Oper	3	EE	
	Absolute.X	INC Oper.X	3	FE	
INX					N V - B D I Z C
Increment index X by one	Implied	INX	1	E8	• •
INY					N V - B D I Z C
Increment index Y by one	Implied	INY	1	C8	• •
JMP					N V - B D I Z C
Jump to new location	Absolute	JMP Oper	3	4C	
	Indirect	JMP (Oper)	3	6C	
JSR					N V - B D I Z C
Jump to new location saving return address	Absolute	JSR Oper	3	20	
LDA					N V - B D I Z C
Load accumulator	Immediate	LDA #Oper	2	A9	• •
with memory	Zero Page	LDA Oper	2	A5	
	Zero Page.X	LDA Oper.X	2	B5	
	Absolute	LDA Oper	3	AD	
	Absolute.X	LDA Oper.X	3	BD	
	Absolute.Y	LDA Oper.Y	3	B9	
	(Indirect.X)	LDA (Oper.X)	2	A1	
	(Indirect).Y	LDA (Oper).Y	2	B1	
LDX					N V - B D I Z C
Load index X	Immediate	LDX #Oper	2	A2	• •
with memory	Zero Page	LDX Oper	2	A6	
	Zero Page.Y	LDX Oper.Y	2	B6	
	Absolute	LDX Oper	3	AE	
	Absolute.Y	LDX Oper.Y	3	BE	
LDY					N V - B D I Z C
Load index Y	Immediate	LDY #Oper	2	A0	• •
with memory	Zero Page	LDY Oper	2	A4	
	Zero Page.X	LDY Oper.X	2	B4	
	Absolute	LDY Oper	3	AC	
	Absolute.X	LDY Oper.X	3	BC	

107

6510 Instruction Codes

Name Description	Addressing Mode	Assembly Language Form	No Bytes	HEX OP Code	Status Register
LSR Shift right one bit (memory or accumulator)	Accumulator Zero Page Zero Page.X Absolute Absolute.X	LSR A LSR Oper LSR Oper.X LSR Oper LSR Oper.X	1 2 2 3 3	4A 46 56 4E 5E	N V - B D I Z C 0 • •
NOP No operation	Implied	NOP	1	EA	N V - B D I Z C
ORA "OR" memory with accumulator	Immediate Zero Page Zero Page.X Absolute Absolute.X Absolute.Y (Indirect.X) (Indirect).Y	ORA #Oper ORA Oper ORA Oper.X ORA Oper ORA Oper.X ORA Oper.Y ORA (Oper.X) ORA (Oper).Y	2 2 2 3 3 3 2 2	09 05 15 0D 1D 19 01 11	N V - B D I Z C • •
PHA Push accumulator on stack	Implied	PHA	1	48	N V - B D I Z C
PHP Push processor status on stack	Implied	PHP	1	08	N V - B D I Z C
PLA Pull accumulator from stack	Implied	PLA	1	68	N V - B D I Z C • •
PLP Pull processor status from stack	Implied	PLP	1	28	N V - B D I Z C • • • • • • • •
ROL Rotate one bit left (memory or accumulator)	Accumulator Zero Page Zero Page.X Absolute Absolute.X	ROL A ROL Oper ROL Oper.X ROL Oper ROL Oper.X	1 2 2 3 3	2A 26 36 2E 3E	N V - B D I Z C • • •
ROR Rotate one bit right (memory or accumulator)	Accumulator Zero Page Zero Page.X Absolute Absolute.X	ROR A ROR Oper ROR Oper.X ROR Oper ROR Oper.X	1 2 2 3 3	6A 66 76 6E 7E	N V - B D I Z C • • •

6510 Instruction Codes

Name Description	Addressing Mode	Assembly Language Form	No Bytes	HEX OP Code	Status Register
RTI Return from interrupt	Implied	RTI	1	40	N V - B D I Z C • • • • • • • •
RTS Return from subroutine	Implied	RTS	1	60	N V - B D I Z C
SBC Subtract memory from accumulator with borrow	Immediate Zero Page Zero Page.X Absolute Absolute.X Absolute.Y (Indirect.X) (Indirect).Y	SBC #Oper SBC Oper SBC Oper.X SBC Oper SBC Oper.X SBC Oper.Y SBC (Oper.X) SBC (Oper).Y	2 2 2 3 3 3 2 2	E9 E5 F5 ED FD F9 E1 F1	N V - B D I Z C • • • •
SEC Set carry flag	Implied	SEC	1	38	N V - B D I Z C 1
SED Set decimal mode	Implied	SED	1	F8	N V - B D I Z C 1
SEI Set interrupt disable status	Implied	SEI	1	78	N V - B D I Z C 1
STA Store accumulator in memory	Zero Page Zero Page.X Absolute Absolute.X Absolute.Y (Indirect.X) (Indirect).Y	STA Oper STA Oper.X STA Oper STA Oper.X STA Oper.Y STA (Oper.X) STA (Oper).Y	2 2 3 3 3 2 2	85 95 8D 9D 99 81 91	N V - B D I Z C
STX Store index X in memory	Zero Page Zero Page.Y Absolute	STX Oper STX Oper.Y STX Oper	2 2 3	86 96 8E	N V - B D I Z C
STY Store index Y in memory	Zero Page Zero Page.X Absolute	STY Oper STY Oper.X STY Oper	2 2 3	84 94 8C	N V - B D I Z C
TAX Transfer accumulator to index X	Implied	TAX	1	AA	N V - B D I Z C • •
TAY Transfer accumulator to index Y	Implied	TAY	1	A8	N V - B D I Z C • •
TSX Transfer stack pointer to index X	Implied	TSX	1	BA	N V - B D I Z C • •

6510 Instruction Codes

Name Description	Addressing Mode	Assembly Language Form	No Bytes	HEX OP Code	Status Register
TXA Transfer index X to accumulator	Implied	TXA	1	BA	N V - B D I Z̲ C ● ●
TXS Transfer index X to stack pointer	Implied	TXS	1	9A	N V - B D I Z C
TYA Transfer index Y to accumulator	Implied	TYA	1	98	N V - B D I Z C ● ●

6510 Microprocessor Operation Codes
in numerical value order

00 — BRK
01 — ORA — (Indirect.X)
02 — ???
03 — ???
04 — ???
05 — ORA — Zero Page
06 — ASL — Zero Page
07 — ???
08 — PHP
09 — ORA — Immediate
0A — ASL — Accumulator
0B — ???
0C — ???
0D — ORA — Absolute
0E — ASL — Absolute
0F — ???
10 — BPL
11 — ORA — (Indirect).Y
12 — ???
13 — ???
14 — ???
15 — ORA — Zero Page.X
16 — ASL — Zero Page.X
17 — ???
18 — CLC
19 — ORA — Absolute.Y
1A — ???
1B — ???
1C — ???
1D — ORA — Absolute.X
1E — ASL — Absolute.X
1F — ???
20 — JSR
21 — AND — (Indirect.X)
22 — ???
23 — ???
24 — BIT — Zero Page
25 — AND — Zero Page
26 — ROL — Zero Page
27 — ???
28 — PLP
29 — AND — Immediate
2A — ROL — Accumulator
2B — ???
2C — BIT — Absolute
2D — AND — Absolute
2E — ROL — Absolute

2F — ???
30 — BMI
31 — AND — (Indirect).Y
32 — ???
33 — ???
34 — ???
35 — AND — Zero Page.X
36 — ROL —Zero Page.X
37 — ???
38 — SEC
39 — AND — Absolute.Y
3A — ???
3B — ???
3C — ???
3D — AND — Absolute.X
3E — ROL — Absolute.X
3F — NOP
40 — RTI
41 — EOR — (Indirect.X)
42 — ???
43 — ???
44 — ???
45 — EOR — Zero Page
46 — LSR — Zero Page
47 — ???
48 — PHA
49 — EOR — Immediate
4A — LSR — Accumulator
4B — ???
4C — JMP — Absolute
4D — EOR — Absolute
4E — LSR — Absolute
4F — ???
50 — BVC
51 — EOR (Indirect).Y
52 — ???
53 — ???
54 — ???
55 — EOR — Zero Page.X
56 — LSR — Zero Page.X
57 — ???
58 — CLI
59 — EOR — Absolute.Y
5A — ???
5B — ???
5C — ???
5D — EOR — Absolute.X

5E — LSR — Sbsolute.X
5F — ???
60 — RTS
61 — ADC — (Indirect.X)
62 — ???
63 — ???
64 — ???
65 — ACD — Zero Page
66 — ROR — Zero Page
67 — ???
68 — PLA
69 — ADC — Immediate
6A — ROR — Accumulator
6B — ???
6C — JMP — Indirect
6D — ADC — Absolute
6E — ROR — Absolute
6F — ???
70 — BVS
71 — ADC — (Indirect).Y
72 — ???
73 — ???
74 — ???
75 — ADC — Zero Page.X
76 — ROR — Zero Page.X
77 — ???
78 — SEI
79 — ADC — Absolute.Y
7A — ???
7B — ???
7C — ???
7D — ADC — Absolute.X
7E — ROR — Absolute.X
7F — ???
80 — ???
81 — STA — (Indirect.X)
82 — ???
83 — ???
84 — STY — Zero Page
85 — STA — Zero Page
86 — STX — Zero Page
87 — ???
88 — DEY
89 — ???
8A — TXA
8B — ???
8C — STY — Absolute

8D — STA — Absolute	B4 — LDY — Zero Page.X	DB — ???
8E — STX — Absolute	B5 — LDA — Zero Page.X	DC — ???
8F — ???	B6 — LDX — Zero Page. Y	DD — CMP — Absolute.X
90 — BCC	B7 — ???	DE — DEC — Absolute.X
91 — STA — (Indirect).Y	B8 — CLV	DF —
92 — ???	B9 — LDA — Absolute.Y	E0 — CPX — Immediate
93 — ???	BA — TSX	E1 — SBC — (Indirect.X)
94 — STY — Zero Page.X	BB — ???	E2 — ???
95 — STA — Zero Page.X	BC — LDY — Absolute.X	E3 — ???
96 — STX — Zero Page.Y	BD — LDA — Absolute.X	E4 — CPX — Zero Page
97 — ???	BE — LDX — Absolute.Y	E5 — SBC — Zero Page
98 — TYA	BF — ???	E6 — INC — Zero Page
99 — STA — Absolute.Y	C0 — CPY — Immediate	E7 — ???
9A — TXS	C1 — CMP — (Indirect.X)	E8 — INX
9B — ???	C2 — ???	E9 — SBC — Immediate
9C — ???	C3 — ???	EA — NOP
9D — STA — Absolute.X	C4 — CPY — Zero Page	EB — ???
9E — ???	C5 — CMP — Zero Page	EC — CPX — Absolute
9F — ???	C6 — DEC — Zero Page	ED — SBC — Absolute
A0 — LDY — Immediate	C7 — ???	EE — INC — Absolute
A1 — LDA — (Indirect.X)	C8 — INY	EF — ???
A2 — LDX — Immediate	C9 — CMP — Immediate	F0 — BEQ
A3 — ???	CA — DEX	F1 — SBC — (Indirect).Y
A4 — LDY — Zero Page	CB — ???	F2 — ???
A5 — LDA — Zero Page	CC — CPY — Absolute	F3 — ???
A6 — LDX — Zero Page	CD — CMP — Absolute	F4 — ???
A7 — ???	CE — DEC — Absolute	F5 — SBC — Zero Page.X
A8 — TAY	CF — ???	F6 — INC — Zero Page.X
A9 — LDA — Immediate	D0 — BNE	F7 — ???
AA — TAX	C1 — CMP — (Indirect) Y	F8 — SED
AB — ???	D2 — ???	F9 — SBC — Absolute.Y
AC — LDY — Absolute	D3 — ???	FA — ???
AD — LDA — Absolute	D4 — ???	FB — ???
AE — LDX — Absolute	D5 — CMP — Zero Page.X	FC — ???
AF — ???	D6 — DEC — Zero Page.X	FD — SBC — Absolute.X
B0 — BCS	D7 — ???	FE — INC — Absolute.X
B1 — LDA — (Indirect).Y	D8 — CLD	FF — ???
B2 — ???	D9 — CMP — Absolute.Y	
B3 — ???	DA — ???	

???Undefined Operation

Appendix 2

6510 Microprocessor Registers

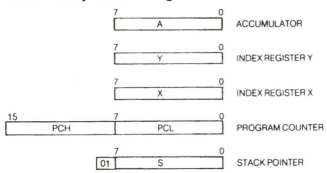

```
 7            0
|      A      |     ACCUMULATOR

 7            0
|      Y      |     INDEX REGISTER Y

 7            0
|      X      |     INDEX REGISTER X

15        7            0
|  PCH    |    PCL     |   PROGRAM COUNTER

         7            0
    |01|    S    |   STACK POINTER
```

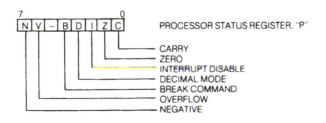

```
 7                   0
| N | V | – | B | D | I | Z | C |    PROCESSOR STATUS REGISTER, "P"
  |   |       |   |   |   |   |____ CARRY
  |   |       |   |   |   |_____ ZERO
  |   |       |   |   |_____ INTERRUPT DISABLE
  |   |       |   |_____ DECIMAL MODE
  |   |       |_____ BREAK COMMAND
  |   |_____ OVERFLOW
  |_____ NEGATIVE
```

Hexadecimal to Decimal Conversion Table
Least Significant Digit

Most Significant Digit

HEX	0 Low Byte	0 High Byte	1 Low Byte	1 High Byte	2 Low Byte	2 High Byte	3 Low Byte	3 High Byte	4 Low Byte	4 High Byte	5 Low Byte	5 High Byte	6 Low Byte	6 High Byte	7 Low Byte	7 High Byte	8 Low Byte	8 High Byte	9 Low Byte	9 High Byte	A Low Byte	A High Byte	B Low Byte	B High Byte	C Low Byte	C High Byte	D Low Byte	D High Byte	E Low Byte	E High Byte	F Low Byte	F High Byte
0	0	0	1	256	2	512	3	768	4	1024	5	1280	6	1536	7	1792	8	2048	9	2304	10	2560	11	2816	12	3072	13	3328	14	3584	15	3840
1	16	4096	17	4352	18	4608	19	4864	20	5120	21	5376	22	5632	23	5888	24	6144	25	6400	26	6656	27	6912	28	7168	29	7424	30	7680	31	7936
2	32	8192	33	8448	34	8704	35	8960	36	9216	37	9472	38	9728	39	9984	40	10240	41	10496	42	10752	43	11008	44	11264	45	11520	46	11776	47	12032
3	48	12288	49	12544	50	12800	51	13056	52	13312	53	13568	54	13824	55	14080	56	14336	57	14592	58	14848	59	15104	60	15360	61	15616	62	15872	63	16128
4	64	16384	65	16640	66	16896	67	17152	68	17408	69	17664	70	17920	71	18176	72	18432	73	18688	74	18944	75	19200	76	19456	77	19712	78	19968	79	20224
5	80	20480	81	20736	82	20992	83	21248	84	21504	85	21760	86	22016	87	22272	88	22528	89	22784	90	23040	91	23296	92	23552	93	23808	94	24064	95	24320
6	96	24576	97	24832	98	25088	99	25344	100	25600	101	25856	102	26112	103	26368	104	26624	105	26880	106	27136	107	27392	108	27648	109	27904	110	28160	111	28416
7	112	28672	113	28928	114	29184	115	29440	116	29696	117	29952	118	30208	119	30464	120	30720	121	30976	122	31232	123	31488	124	31744	125	32000	126	32256	127	32512
8	128	32768	129	33024	130	33280	131	33536	132	33792	133	34048	134	34304	135	34560	136	34816	137	35072	138	35328	139	35584	140	35840	141	36096	142	36352	143	36608
9	144	36864	145	37120	146	37376	147	37632	148	37888	149	38144	150	38400	151	38656	152	38912	153	39168	154	39424	155	39680	156	39936	157	40192	158	40448	159	40704
A	160	40960	161	41216	162	41472	163	41728	164	41984	165	42240	166	42496	167	42752	168	43008	169	43264	170	43520	171	43776	172	44032	173	44288	174	44544	175	44800
B	176	45056	177	45312	178	45568	179	45824	180	46080	181	46336	182	46592	183	46848	184	47104	185	47360	186	47616	187	47872	188	48128	189	48384	190	48640	191	48896
C	192	49152	193	49408	194	49664	195	49920	196	50176	197	50432	198	50688	199	50944	200	51200	201	51456	202	51712	203	51968	204	52224	205	52480	206	52736	207	52992
D	208	53248	209	53504	210	53760	211	54016	212	54272	213	54528	214	54784	215	55040	216	55296	217	55552	218	55808	219	56064	220	56320	221	56576	222	56832	223	57088
E	224	57344	225	57600	226	57856	227	58112	228	58368	229	58624	230	58880	231	59136	232	59392	233	59648	234	59904	235	60160	236	60416	237	60672	238	60928	239	61184
F	240	61440	241	61696	242	61952	243	62208	244	62464	245	62720	246	62976	247	63232	248	63488	249	63744	250	64000	251	64256	252	64512	253	64768	254	65024	255	65280

114

Appendix 3

Hexadecimal to Decimal Conversion Table

This table can be used to convert up to four digit hex numbers to decimal.

How to use the table:

1. Divide the number into groups of two digits,
   e.g. $F17B → F1   7B
       $2A   → 2A

2. Take the low byte of the number (from above 7B or 2A) and look it up in the chart. Find the most significant digit (7) in the column on the left, find the least significant digit (8) in the row along the top, and find the box in which the row (7) and the column (B) cross. In that box you will find 2 numbers, ⎸123 31488⎹ . These are the values of 7B in the low byte and the high byte. Since we are looking up the low byte, take the value 123. Now find the location of the high byte of our number (F1) on the chart. The box here contains ⎸241 61696⎹ . Since we are now dealing with the high byte, take the value 61696 from that box and add it to the value we found earlier for the low byte 123.

   61696
   + 123
   _____
   61819   which is the decimal value of $F17B
   _____

   NOTE: to find the decimal value of a two digit number, e.g. 2A, look it up in the chart taking the low byte value (42). For a one digit number, e.g. E, create a two digit number by adding a leading zero (ØE), and similarly make three digit numbers four digits with a leading zero.

Relative Branch Tables   and
Two's Complement Numbering tables

FORWARD RELATIVE BRANCH   POSITIVE NUMBERS

low\hi	0	1	2	3	4	5	6	7	8	9	A	B	C	D	E	F
0	0	1	2	3	4	5	6	7	8	9	10	11	12	13	14	15
1	16	17	18	19	20	21	22	23	24	25	26	27	28	29	30	31
2	32	33	34	35	36	37	38	39	40	41	42	43	44	45	46	47
3	48	49	50	51	52	53	54	55	56	57	58	59	60	61	62	63
4	64	65	66	67	68	69	70	71	72	73	74	75	76	77	78	79
5	80	81	82	83	84	85	86	87	88	89	90	91	92	93	94	95
6	96	97	98	99	100	101	102	103	104	105	106	107	108	109	110	111
7	112	113	114	115	116	117	118	119	120	121	122	123	124	125	126	127

BACKWARD RELATIVE BRANCH   NEGATIVE NUMBERS

low\hi	0	1	2	3	4	5	6	7	8	9	A	B	C	D	E	F
8	128	127	126	125	124	123	122	121	120	119	118	117	116	115	114	113
9	112	111	110	109	108	107	106	105	104	103	102	101	100	99	98	97
A	96	95	94	93	92	91	90	89	88	87	86	85	84	83	82	81
B	80	79	78	77	76	75	74	73	72	71	70	69	68	67	66	65
C	64	63	62	61	60	59	58	57	56	55	54	53	52	51	50	49
D	48	47	46	45	44	43	42	41	40	39	38	37	36	35	34	33
E	32	31	30	29	28	27	26	25	24	23	22	21	20	19	18	17
F	16	15	14	13	12	11	10	9	8	7	6	5	4	3	2	1

Appendix 4

Relative Branch and Two's Complement Numbering Tables

1. To calculate relative branches, locate the address immediately after the location of the branch instruction. Count the number of bytes from there to where you want the branch to end up. If the destination is before the first byte, use the backward branch table and if not, use the forward branch table. Look up the displacement (the number you counted) in the body of the appropriate chart and read off the high and low digits of the branch from the sides. This can also be used in reverse, by looking up a branch on the sides to find the displacement taken in the body of the chart.

2. To convert from a signed decimal number between −128 and 127 to a hex two's complement number, find your decimal number in the body of the appropriate chart (positives and negatives) and read off the hex two's complement number from the sides (high digit, low digit). The reverse process (two's complement hex to signed decimal) is simply a matter of finding the high digit on the column on the left, the low digit on the top row, reading off the number where the row and column meet, and if in the negative chart make the number negative.

COMMODORE 64 MEMORY MAP

$FFFF	(65535)
	KERNAL ROM
$E000	(57344)
$DC00	CIA 1, CIA 2
	(55320)
	Colour Ram Nibbles
$D800	(55296)
	VIC II SOUND
$D000	(53248)
	4K RAM
$C000	(49152)
	BASIC INTERPRETER ROM
$A000	(40960)
$8000 (32768)	
$4000 (16384)	BASIC User RAM
$2000 (8192)	
$1FF	(511)
$100	STACK
$0000	ZERO-PAGE

Characters ROM D

8K RAM A
4K RAM B

8K RAM C
EXROM 8K ROM Cartridge

MEMORY LOCATION $0001

VALUE	MEMORY FORMAT
xxxxx111	Normal (Not A, B, C or D)
xxxxx110	A
xxxxx101	C
xxxxx100	A, B, C
xxxxx011	D
xxxxx010	A, D
xxxxx001	C, D
xxxxx000	A, C, D (Not B)

118

Appendix 5

Commodore 64 Memory Map

You have heard that the Commodore 64 has 64K of RAM, and we know that in a two byte address we can only access 64K. Where then are those ROM routines which hold character sets, BASIC and the operating system? In the C64 there is 20K of ROM as well as the 64K of RAM. In certain areas there is RAM (or RAM and the Character Generator ROM) 'mapped' onto normal memory. This means that normal memory in those places can be switched out and the extra memory can be switched in instead.

The 'switch' which performs this task is located at address $0001. The first three bits of $0001 are used to define which memory is used according to the table included. We have already used this switching in and out of memory to read from the Character Generator ROM in Chapter 8. Refer to it for the method used.

VIC-II CHIP REGISTER MAP

Reg. #	7	6	5	4	3	2	1	0	
0	Sprite# 0			x — position					
1	Sprite# 0			y — position					
2	Sprite# 1			x — position					
3	Sprite# 1			y — position					
4	Sprite# 2			x — position					
5	Sprite# 2			y — position					
6	Sprite# 3			x — position					
7	Sprite# 3			y — position					
8	Sprite# 4			x — position					
9	Sprite# 4			y — position					
10	Sprite# 5			x — position					
11	Sprite# 5			y — position					
12	Sprite# 6			x — position					
13	Sprite# 6			y — position					
14	Sprite# 7			x — position					
15	Sprite# 7			y — position					
16	Sprite #7	Sprite #6	Sprite #5	Sprite #4	Sprite #3	Sprite #2	Sprite #1	Sprite #0	MSB of x — position
17	RASTER MSB	EXTENDED Colour	Bit map	Display enable	Screen height	—	Vertical Scroll	—	Mode / y — scroll
18	Raster register								
19	Light pen — x								
20	Light pen — y								
21	Sprite #7	Sprite #6	Sprite #5	Sprite #4	Sprite #3	Sprite #2	Sprite #1	Sprite #0	Sprite enable
22	—	—	Reset Multi	Multi colour	Screen width	—	Horizontal scroll	—	Multi colour / x scroll
23	Sprite #7	Sprite #6	Sprite #5	Sprite #4	Sprite #3	Sprite #2	Sprite #1	Sprite #0	Sprite y — expand
24	Screen location				Character base				
25	IRQ	—	—	—	Light pen	Sprite-Sprite collision	Sprite-b'gnd collision	Raster	Interrupt register
26	IRQ	—	—	—	Light pen	Sprite-Sprite collision	Sprite b'gnd collision	Raster	Interupt enable
27	Sprite #7	Sprite #6	Sprite #5	Sprite #4	Sprite #3	Sprite #2	Sprite #1	Sprite #0	Sprite — background priority
28	Sprite #7	Sprite #6	Sprite #5	Sprite #4	Sprite #3	Sprite #2	Sprite #1	Sprite #0	Sprite multicolour select
29	Sprite #7	Sprite #6	Sprite #5	Sprite #4	Sprite #3	Sprite #2	Sprite #1	Sprite #0	Sprite x — expand
30	Sprite #7	Sprite #6	Sprite #5	Sprite #4	Sprite #3	Sprite #2	Sprite #1	Sprite #0	Sprite to Sprite collision
31	Sprite #7	Sprite #6	Sprite #5	Sprite #4	Sprite #3	Sprite #2	Sprite #1	Sprite #0	Sprite to background collision
32	Screen border Colour								
33	Background Colour #0								
34	Background Colour #1								
35	Background Colour #2								
36	Background Colour #3								
37	Sprite multicolour #0								
38	Sprite multicolour #1								
39	Sprite #0 Colour								
40	Sprite #1 Colour								
41	Sprite #2 Colour								
42	Sprite #3 Colour								
43	Sprite #4 Colour								
44	Sprite #5 Colour								
45	Sprite #6 Colour								
46	Sprite #7 Colour								

Appendix 6

The Screen Chip

The VIC-II screen chip is an extremely flexible display controller which handles all the text, graphics and sprites on the Commodore 64.

The chip addresses 16K of memory, in other words, all the graphics and colour memory information must be stored within ONE of the four 16K 'banks' of memory which make up the 64K of memory within the Commodore. To choose the bank you want, you set the appropriate bits in the I/O ports of the CIA#2 at address $DD00 (see Appendix 8). First however, the data direction port must be set.

The BASIC statement to do this is as follows:

POKE 56578, PEEK (56578) OR 3

The BASIC statement to select the video bank is as follows:

POKE 56576, (PEEK(56576) AND 252) OR (3 − BANK)

where the value of BANK depends on the following table:

Value of Bank	Bits	Bank	Starting Location		VIC-II Chip Range
0	00	0	$0000	0	0 − 16383 (Default bank)
1	01	1	$4000	16384	16384 − 32767
2	10	2	$8000	32768	32768 − 49151
3	11	3	$C000	41952	49152 − 65535

The VIC-II chip is normally set to look at the first 16K of memory (Bank 0). The start of the VIC-II memory will be referred to as the BASE address.

VIC-II Chip

Registers 0 − 15 at $D000 − $D00F (53272 − 53287)
sprite 0 − 7 position registers.

Each sprite has two position registers X and Y which hold a value equal to the visible screen but relative to the raster beam (the electron beam inside the T.V. which creates the picture). (See sprite positioning chart.)

It is possible to create a sprite which is not on the visible screen but still has all the functions of a sprite, e.g. collision testing (see later). This

121

is useful in certain games where off-screen collisions may be an interesting feature.

You will notice that the Y values can all fit into 8 bits (are less than 256), but the X co-ordinates can be larger — up to $158 (334) on screen. For the solution to this problem see Register 16.

Register 16 at $D010 (53288)

Register 16 contains the most significant bit of each of the 8 sprite X co-ordinate sprite position registers. This allows for X positions greater than 255.

Register 17 at $D011 (53289)

BITS 0 - 2 VERTICAL SCROLL

The value in these bits (from 0 - 7) shifts the screen up or down by an equivalent number of pixels. By incrementing this three bit value and scrolling the screen as it jumps from one extreme to the other, you can create a smooth vertical scroll which is extremely impressive in many games programs.

BIT 3 SCREEN HEIGHT

This bit controls whether 24 or 25 rows of text will be displayed. It is most often used in conjunction with the vertical scroll to eliminate the 'gap' produced when scrolling pixel by pixel.

BIT 4 DISPLAYENABLE

This bit controls whether anything is displayed or not. It can be used to quickly blank the screen or to blank during annoying output, e.g. on cassette loads. (This does not change the data to be displayed; it just stops it being shown till its value is changed again.)

BIT 5 BIT MAP

This bit switches the VIC-II into and out of bit map mode. For a description of bit map mode see later.

BIT 6 EXTENDED COLOUR

This bit switches the VIC-II into and out of extended colour mode. In this mode extra colours can be used on text or graphics at the price of a loss of printable characters or, alternately, horizontal resolution.

BIT 7 MSB RASTER REGISTER

This is the most significant bit of the raster register (number 18. $D012)

Register 18 at $D012 (53290)

RASTER REGISTER

The raster register, if read, contains the number of the current line which is being drawn on the screen. Machine code programs are so fast that several thousand of them occur in the time it takes for the television to draw one screen (the screen is completely redrawn fifty times every second). A write (or store) into the raster register will cause an interrupt to be sent to the microprocessor every time the raster beam draws the line specified in the store (if the interrupt register at $D01A has been set to enable raster interrupts).

This can be used to extend the capabilities of the VIC-II by swapping video banks, screen modes, sprite or character data in mid screen, thereby having twice or several times (several interrupts) the number of features.

Register 19 – 20 at $D013 – $D014 (53291 – 53292)
Light Pen X and Y

Register 21 at $D015 (53293)
Register 21 enables (turns on) each of the 8 sprites 0 – 7 by turning on the equivalent bit in the register.

Register 22 at $D016 (53294)

Bits 0 – 2   Horizontal Scroll
             See Vertical Scroll
Bit 3   Screen width
             See screen height — width varies between 38 or 40 characters.
Bits 4 – 5   Set and Reset Mulicolour mode
             Similar to extended colour mode, see later.
Bits 6 – 7   unused.

Register 23 at $D017 (53295)
Register 23 expands by a factor of two (doubles) the height of each of the sprites 0 – 7 by turning on the equivalent bit in the register.

Register 24 at $D018 (53296)
This register defines the location of screen memory, colour memory or character memory depending on the mode you are in. This will be explained further when the various modes are discussed.

Register 25 – 26 at $D019 to $D01A (53297 - 53298)
Turning on a bit in register 26 will enable an interrupt to occur, e.g. turning on bit zero will allow an interrupt to occur when the raster beam draws the line specified in the raster register. When an

interrupt is received you can check the value of register 25 to determine what sort of interrupt occurred. The value read from here must be echoed back into register 25 before the next interrupt will occur.

Register 27 at $D01B (53299)

Used to control whether individual sprites appear in front of or behind other data displayed on the screen.

Register 28 at $D01C (53300)

Used to make any sprite appear in multicolour mode.

Register 29 at $D01D (53301)

Horizontal expand (double). See register 23

Register 30 to 31 at $D01E to $D01F (53302 55303)

If the interrupt enable register at $D01A is set for sprite-sprite collisions, or for sprite-background collisions, these registers will define which sprites will cause an interrupt on collision and which will not.

Registers 32 – 46 at $D020 to $D02E (53304 to 53318)

Self explanatory.

Standard Character Mode

In standard character mode our screen memory is 1000 bytes long. Each byte represents one of 255 characters. The color of each byte is defined by colour RAM which is 1000 locations from $D800 – $DBE8 (55296 – 56295). Each piece of memory in colour RAM is on 4 bits long and can only store numbers from 0 to 15 (see table of colour values).

Both screen memory and character memory may be defined anywhere within the 16K video bank in use by storing values in the VIC-II register #24. The address of screen memory is defined by the top 4 bits (7 – 4) of register 24. Four bits specify a number between 0 and 16, so Screen address = Base address + 1024 × Top four bits register 24.

By changing the address of character memory to a RAM address we can redefine our character set (or just swap sets) (see Chapter 8 for details on character sets). Bits 3 – 1 define the location of the character set in memory. This is a 3 bit number (0 – 7), therefore:

character address = Base Address + 1024 × Bits 3 – 1 register 24

To access the ROM character set, set bits 3 – 1 to 010 for Set 1 or 011 for Set 2. Bit 0 of register 24 at $D018 is ignored.

Multicolour Character Mode

This is the same as standard character mode except for the way in which characters are defined (see Chapter 8). In standard mode, one

124

bit is equivalent to one pixel. In multicolour mode, two bits appear as one pixel but extra colours can be shown. Hence we get multicoloured characters of 4 × 8 pixels (each byte formerly in 8 bits is now in 4 bit pairs).

A bit pair containing 00 displays background colour #0
A bit pair containing 01 displays background colour #1
A bit pair containing 10 displays background colour #2
A bit pair containing 11 displays colour from the lower 3 bits of colour memory.

Setting the fourth bit of colour memory makes that character position on the screen multicolour, while clearing it leaves that position in standard character mode.

Extended Background Colour Mode

This is similar to multicolour mode except that instead of losing resolution we reduce the number of different characters we can print from 255 to 63. This means that the top two bits of every screen byte can be used to specify one of the background colour registers on the VIC-II chip. Therefore each character can take any one of four background colours. The foreground is still specified by colour RAM.

If the top two bits of a screen memory byte
= 00 → background colour #0
= 01 → background colour #1
= 10 → background colour #2
= 11 → background colour #3

Bit Map Mode

The technicalities of bit map mode have been discussed in Chapter 8. The bit mapped screen takes up 8K of memory and it must start on an 8K boundary as defined by the low bits of register 24 at $D018. The top four bits define an area of memory which is used as colour memory. For each character position you can display two colours — one in the top four bits of the colour memory specified and the other in the low four bits.

Multicolour Bit Map Mode

Similarly to multicolour character mode, here we take a loss of resolution in return for extra colour capacity. Each byte is again divided into bit pairs which are displayed as follows:

00 → background colour #0
01 → lower 4 bits of specified colour memory
10 → upper 4 bits of specified colour memory
11 → four bits of colour RAM.

TABLE OF COLOUR VALUES

Ø Black	4 Purple	8 Orange	12 Grey 2
1 White	5 Green	9 Brown	13 Light Green
2 Red	6 Blue	10 Light Red	14 Light Blue
3 Cyan	7 Yellow	11 Grey 1	15 Grey 3

COLOUR MIX CHART

Character Colour

	Ø	1	2	3	4	5	6	7	8	9	10	11	12	13	14	15
Ø	X	✓	X	✓	✓	•	X	✓	✓	x	✓	✓	✓	✓	✓	✓
1	✓	X	✓	X	✓	✓	✓	X	•	✓	•	✓	✓	X	✓	✓
2	X	✓	X	X	•	X	X	✓	✓	X	✓	X	X	X	X	•
3	✓	X	X	X	X	•	✓	X	X	X	X	•	X	X	•	X
4	✓	•	X	X	X	X	X	X	X	X	X	X	X	X	X	•
5	✓	•	X	•	X	X	X	X	X	X	X	X	•	X	✓	•
6	•	✓	X	✓	X	X	X	X	X	X	X	X	X	X	•	✓
7	✓	X	✓	X	X	X	•	X	•	✓	•	✓	✓	X	X	X
8	•	✓	✓	X	X	X	X	✓	X	✓	X	X	X	X	X	•
9	X	✓	X	X	X	X	X	✓	✓	X	✓	X	X	X	X	✓
10	•	•	✓	X	X	X	X	•	X	✓	X	X	X	X	X	•
11	✓	✓	X	•	X	X	X	✓	X	X	X	X	✓	✓	•	✓
12	✓	✓	•	X	X	X	•	X	X	•	X	✓	X	X	X	✓
13	✓	X	X	X	X	✓	•	X	X	X	X	✓	X	X	X	X
14	✓	✓	X	✓	X	X	✓	X	X	X	X	•	X	X	X	•
15	✓	✓	✓	X	•	•	✓	X	X	•	•	✓	✓	X	•	X

✓ Good Mix

• Fair Mix

X Poor Mix

126

SPRITE POSITIONING CHART

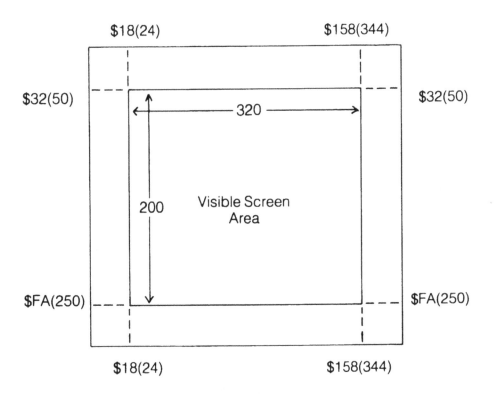

CHARACTER GENERATOR ROM

ADDRESS		CONTENTS
HEX	DECIMAL	
D000 - D1FF	53248	Upper case characters
D200 - D3FF	53760	Graphics characters
D400 - D5FF	54272	Reversed upper case characters
D600 - D7FF	54784	Reversed graphics characters
D800 - D9FF	55296	Lower case characters
DA00 - DBFF	55808	Upper case & graphics characters
DC00 - DDFF	56320	Reversed lower case characters
DE00 - DFFF	56832	Reversed upper case & graphics characters

NOTE: see Appendix 00 on memory mapping to see how to access this memory.

127

Appendix 7
The Sound Chip

The Sound Chip Registers

	Bit significance								Register usage (Voice-1)
REG No.	b7	b6	b5	b4	b3	b2	b1	b0	
0	NL_7	NL_6	NL_5	NL_4	NL_3	NL_2	NL_1	NL_0	Low byte of note frequency
1	NH_7	NH_6	NH_5	NH_4	NH_3	NH_2	NH_1	NH_0	High byte of note frequency
2	PL_7	PL_6	PL_5	PL_4	PL_3	PL_2	PL_1	PL_0	Low byte of pulse width
3	—	—	—	—	PH_3	PH_2	PH_1	PH_0	High byte of pulse width
4	Noise ⊓⊔ /\/\ /\/\				TEST	RING MOD	SYNC	GATE	Wave form control
5	A_3	A_2	A_1	A_0	D_3	D_2	D_1	D_0	Attack/decay for envelope
6	S_3	S_2	S_1	S_0	R_3	R_2	R_1	R_0	Sustain/release for envelope

Voices 2 and 3 are mirror images of the above except that they are stored in registers 7 to 13 and 14 to 20 respectively.

	Bit significance								Register usage (Filter)
21	—	—	—	—	—	CL_2	CL_1	CL_0	Low cutoff frequency
22	CH_7	CH_6	CH_5	CH_4	CH_3	CH_2	CH_1	CH_0	High cutoff frequency
23	R_3	R_2	R_1	R_0	F_{EX}	$F3$	$F2$	$F1$	Filter switches and resonance
24	3OFF	HP	BP	LP	V_3	V_2	V_1	V_0	Filter modes and volume

	Bit significance								Register usage (Misc.)
25	P_7	P_6	P_5	P_4	P_3	P_2	P_1	P_0	Paddle · x
26	P_7	P_6	P_5	P_4	P_3	P_2	P_1	P_0	Paddle · y
27	O_7	O_6	O_5	O_4	O_3	O_2	O_1	O_0	Oscillator - 3 output
28	E_7	E_6	E_5	E_4	E_3	E_2	E_1	E_0	Envelope - 3 output

NOTE: The sound chip registers are accessed via memory locations $D400 to $D41C (54272 to 54300).

Playing Tunes

The most practical way of writing a BASIC program to play a tune is to store the tune as data. For simple tunes, only two items of data are needed: the note frequency and the duration of each note to be played. The following steps are necessary when writing a BASIC program to play a simple tune.

1. Simplify the addressing of all sound register memory locations to be used by assigning a variable name to each location.

2. Clear the sound chip by setting all the sound chip registers to zero.

3. POKE the attack/decay registers and the sustain/release registers with the attack, decay, release values chosen from the table in the envelope setting.

4. Load the volume register with the maximum volume (i.e. 15)

5. Set up a program loop that does the following:
   Read the frequency of the next note and the duration of the note. If there are no more frequencies then end. Otherwise, load the frequency registers with their data. Turn on the waveform and the GATE bit (see register map). Use a FOR NEXT loop to loop for the duration. Turn off the gate bit. Use a FOR NEXT loop to create a suitable pause (say 50 counts). Go back and do it again.

6. Use the note table at the end of this chapter and durations using 1000 as an approximation of about 1 sec.

7. End data with three negative values to signal end-of-tune. Your program should look similar to the following:

```
5 REM * TUNE *
10 CHIP=54272 : C=CHIP
20 NL(0)=C+0:NH(0)=C+1:WK0)=C+4:AD(0)=C+5:SR(0)
   =C+6:VOLUME=C+24
30 FOR REG=CHIPTOCHIP+24:POKEREG,0:NEXT
40 POKE AD(0),64+9 : POKE SR(0),240+0
50 POKE VOLUME,15
60 READ F,DUR : IF F<0 THEN POKE WK0),0:END
65 DUR=DUR*20
70 NH(1)=INT(F/256):NL(1)=F-NH(1)*256:POKENH(0),
   NH(1):POKENL(0),NL(1)
80 POKE WK0),32+1:REM ADD 1 FOR GATE
90 FOR COUNT=1 TO DUR :NEXT COUNT
100 POKE WK0),32:REM TURN OFF GATE
```

129

```
110 FOR PAUSE=1 TO 50 :NEXT
120 GOTO 60
310 DATA 4820,8,6420,8,6420,12,6068,4,6420,8,
    8100,8,8100,8,7220,8,9637,8
320 DATA 9637,8,9637,12,8581,4,8100,8,7220,8,
    8100,16,4820,8,6420,8,6420,12
330 DATA 6068,4,6420,8,8100,8,8100,8,7220,8,
    9637,8,7220,8,7220,12,6068,4
340 DATA 6068,8,5396,8,4820,16
399 DATA -1,-1,-1
READY.
```

Registers 0 and 1 (Location $D400 and $D401) (54272 and 54273)

(Low and high bytes of note frequency)

These two registers form a two byte value corresponding to the frequency of a note played. To obtain the actual frequency of the note being played, multiply the two byte value by 0.059604645.

Registers 2 and 3 (Location $D402 and $D403) (54274 and 54275)

(Low and high bytes of pulse width of pulse wave)

These two registers form a 12-bit value corresponding to the pulse width of the pulse wave. The width of the low pulse of the pulse cycle as a percentage of the width of the pulse cycle is given by the following formula:

Low pulse width = (12-bit value/40.95)% of the pulse cycle; where a low pulse width of 0% or 100% is a constant DC signal (i.e. zero output) and a low pulse width of 50% is a square wave.

Register 4 (Location $D404) (54276)

(Waveform control)

This register serves several functions where each bit serves a separate function.

Bit 0 (Gate Bit):

The gate bit controls the envelope generator. Setting this bit to a 1 turns on the ADSR envelope and begins the envelope cycle at the attack stage, goes on to the decay stage and finally the sustain. The sound will continue at the sustain level until the gate bit is set to zero, in which case envelope control will continue to the release stage. If the gate bit is set to zero before the sustain stage has been reached, then envelope control will jump to the release stage.

Bit-1 (Sync Bit):

Setting the sync bit to 1 causes the waveform from voice 3 to be syncronized with voice 1. Varying the frequency of voice 3 will change the overall waveform output of voice 1.

Bit-2 (Ring Mod Bit):
Setting the ring mod bit to a 1 replaces the triangle waveform of voice 1 with a 'ring-modulated' combination of oscillators 1 and 3 for giving the output a bell type sound. Varying the frequency of oscillator 3 causes changes in the overall waveform output of voice 1.

Bit-3 (Test Bit):
Mainly used for testing, this bit, when set to 1, causes oscillator 1 to reset to 0 and lock there until the bit is reset. However, it can be used to synchronize oscillator 1 to an external device.

Bit-4 (Triangle Waveform):
When set to 1, this bit selects the triangle waveform to be used for output of oscillator 1.

Bit-5 (Sawtooth Waveform):
When set to 1, this bit selects the sawtooth waveform.

Bit-6 (Pulse Waveform):
When set to 1, selects the pulse waveform.

Bit-7 (Noise Waveform):
When set to 1, selects the noise waveform.

Register 5 (Location $D405) (54277)
(Attack/decay)
This register is used to select the attack and decay rate for voice 1's ADSR envelope.

Bits 4 − 7 (Attack Rate):
Selects an attack rate from 0 − 240 where the attack times range from 2ms to 8s.

Bits 0 − 3 (Decay Rate):
Select a decay rate from 0 − 15 where the decay times range from 6ms to 24s.

Register 6 (Location $D406) (54278)
(Sustain/release)
This register is used to select the sustain level and release rate for voice 1's ADSR envelope.

Bits 4 − 7 (Sustain Rate):
Selects a sustain level from 0 − 240 where the sustain setting is a proportion of the volume setting. To obtain the actual sustain volume, use the following equation:
Sustain volume = (volume setting *sustain setting) / 240

131

Bits 0 – 3 (Release Rate):
Selects a release rate from 0 – 15 where the release times range from 6ms to 24s.

Registers 7 – 13 (Locations $D407 to $D40D) (54279 to 54285)

(Voice 2)
These registers are functionally indentical to registers 0 – 6 (voice 1) with the following exceptions:

1. SYNC – Synchronizes oscillator 2 with oscillator 1.

2. RING MOD – Replaces the triangle output of oscillator 2 with the ring modulated combination of oscillators 2 and 1.

Registers 14 – 20 (Locations $D40E to $D414) (54286 to 54292)

(Voice 3)
These registers are functionally identical to registers 0 – 6 (voice 1) and registers 7 – 13 (voice 2) with the following exceptions:

1. SYNC – Syncronizes oscillator 3 with oscillator 2.

2. RING MOD – Replaces the triangle output of oscillator 3 with the ring modulated combination of oscillators 3 and 2.

Registers 21 and 22 (Locations $D415 and $D416) (54293 and 54294)

(Cutoff frequency)
These two registers form an 11-bit value corresponding to the cutoff (or centre) frequency of the programmable filter. They select a cutoff value of 0 – 262 where the cutoff frequency ranges from 30 Hz – 12KHz.

Register 23 (Location $D417) (54295)

(Resonance/filter)
This register is used to select the resonance and filter switches.

Bit-0 (Filter Switch 1):
When set to 1, voice 1 is sent through the filters before output. When set to 0, voice 1 is sent directly to output.

Bits 1 and 2 (Filter Switches 2 and 3):
Same as bit Ø but for voices 2 and 3 respectively.

Bit-3 (Filter Switch EXT):
Same as bit Ø but for external audio input.

Bits 4 — 7 (Resonance Setting):
This register forms a 4-bit value corresponding to the resonance setting of the programmable filter. They select resonance settings that range from 16 — 24Ø in steps of 16. The resonance acts on a small band of frequencies around the selected cutoff frequency.

Register 24 (Location $D418) (54296)

(Voice 3's switch/filter modes/volume setting)

Bits Ø — 3 (Volume Setting):
These four bits are used to select volume settings which range from Ø — 15. This is a master volume control, however each voice may be varied by either setting a large attack and setting the gate bit to Ø during attack, or by setting a different sustain level for each voice, thus achieving different volume levels for each voice within the absolute level set by the above four bits.

Bits 4 — 6 (Filter Modes):
These three bits are used to select the filter modes for the programmable filter. Bit 4 selects the 'lowpass' filter, bit 5 selects the 'bandpass' filter and bit 6 selects the 'highpass' filter. More than one filter may be selected at one time. For example, a 'notch reject' filter can be set up by selecting the lowpass and highpass filters.

Bit-7 (Voice 3 Switch):
Setting this bit to 1 causes voice 3 output to be disconnected without effecting any of the voice 3 controls. This switch is used when voice 3 is used to control another voice and the output of voice 3 is not needed.

Registers 25 and 26 (Location $D419 and $D41A) (54297 and 54298)

(Paddles)
These registers allow the microprocessor to read the positions of a pair of paddles connected to port-1 (labelled port-2 on computer casing). The paddles should give readings of Ø for minimum resistance and 255 for maximum resistance. By reading these registers and writing their contents to other sound chip registers, it is possible to control the sound chip with the paddles.

Register 27 (Location $D41B) (54299)

(Oscillator 3 output)

This register allows the microprocessor to read the waveform output of voice 3 where any waveform will produce values between Ø and 255. For example, if the sawtooth is selected, register 27 will output incrementing values from Ø to 255 at a rate depending on the frequency setting of voice 3.

Register 28 (Location $D41C) (543ØØ)

(Envelope 3 output)

Same as register 27, but this register allows the microprocessor to read the envelope output of voice 3.

Complex Interface Adapter
(CIA) Interface Chip
Register Map

Reg	Name		#1 $DC00 - $DC0F Purpose	#2 $DD00 - $DD0F Purpose
0	PRA	Peripheral Data Reg A	Keyboard, Joysticks, Paddle, Light Pen	Serial Bus, RS232, Memory Control
1	PRB	Peripheral Data Reg B	Keyboard, Joysticks, Paddles	RS232, User Port
2	DDRA	Data Direction Reg A	To define which bits of A are read	To define which bits of A are read
3	DDRB	Data Direction Reg B	To define which bits of B are read	To define which bits of B are read
4	TA LO	Timer A Low Register	System Interrupt Timer	User Timer
5	TA HI	Timer A High Register	System Interrupt Timer	User Timer
6	TB LO	Timer B Low Register	System Interrupt Timer	User Timer
7	TB HI	Timer B High Register	System Interrupt Timer	User Timer
8	TOD 10THS	10THS of Seconds Register	System Clock	User Clock
9	TOD SEC	Seconds Register	System Clock	User Clock
A	TOD MIN	Minutes Register	System Clock	User Clock
B	TOD HR	Hours — AM/PM Register	System Clock	User Clock
C	SDR	Serial Data Register	Serial I/O	Serial I/O
D	ICR	Interrupt Control Register	System Interrupt Control	User Interrupt Control
E	CRA	Control Reg A	System Timer A Controller	User Timer A Controller
F	CRB	Control Reg B	System Timer B Controller	User Timer B Controller

136

Appendix 8

Complex Interface Adapter
(CIA) Interface Chip

There are two CIA chips on the Commodore 64 and generally one is ised for system functions and one for user functions. Each chip (#1 and #2) has 16 registers mapped onto memory from $DC00 – $DC0F (#1) and $DD00 – $DD0F (#2).

Registers 0 – 3

These four registers are combined to create two 'bidirectional' I/O registers. Registers 0 and 1 contain the data for this I/O while registers 2 and 3 contain masks to control the movement of this data. If register 2 contains $E0 (11100000) as a mask only the top 3 bits of register 0 will be effective. (For a Read (LDA Reg 0) bits 5, 6, 7 will be inputs, For a Write (STA Reg 0) bits 5, 6, 7 will be outputs). The same applies for register 3 and register 1.

CIA #1

	Register 0	$DC00 (56320)
Write	bits 0 - 7	keyboard scan column
Read	bits 0 - 7	light pen
	OR	
	bits 6 - 7	read paddles
	bits 2 - 3	paddle fire buttons
	OR	
	bit 4	Joystick 0 fire button
	bits 0 - 3	Joystick 0 direction
		(See Joystick direction table)

	Register 1	$DC01 (56321)
Write	bits 6 - 7	Timer A and B toggle
Read	bits 0 - 7	Keyboard scan Row values
	OR	
	bits 2 - 3	Paddle fire buttons
	OR	
	bit 4	Joystick 1 fire buttons
	bits 0 - 3	Joystick 1 direction
		(See Joystick direction table)

Joystick Direction Table

Bits		0 - 3		Direction
Ø	Ø	Ø	Ø	None
Ø	Ø	Ø	1	Up
Ø	Ø	1	Ø	Down
Ø	Ø	1	1	—
Ø	1	Ø	Ø	Left
Ø	1	Ø	1	Up and Left
Ø	1	1	Ø	Down and Left
Ø	1	1	1	—
1	Ø	Ø	Ø	Right
1	Ø	Ø	1	Up and Right
1	Ø	1	Ø	Down and Right

CIA #1

7	6	5	4	3	2	1	Ø
—	—	—	FIRE	RIGHT	LEFT	DOWN	UP

(Bits used by location 56320 and 56321 for joystick ports 1 and 2 respectively).

CIA #2

	Register 0	$DD00 (56576)
Write	bit 5	serial bus data output
	bit 4	serial bus clock pulse output
	bit 3	serial bus ATN signal output
	bit 2	RS-232 data output (user port)
	bit 0 - 1	VIC-II chip memory select
		(see Appendix — VIC-II bank select)
Read	bit 7	serial bus data input
	bit 6	serial bit clock pulse input

	Register 1	$DD01 (56577)
	User Port	
	OR	
	bit 7 - RS-232	Data set ready
	bit 6 - RS-232	Clear to send
	bit 4 - RS-232	Carrier detect
	bit 3 - RS-232	Ring indicator
	bit 2 - RS-232	Data terminal ready
	bit 1 - RS-232	Request to send
	bit 0 - RS-232	Received data

The following registers are used similarly on CIA #1 and CIA #2 and so are listed together.

Registers 2 - 3

Data direction registers for registers 0 and 1.
CIA #1 $DC02 and $DC03 (56322 - 56323) for $DC00 and $DD01
CIA #2 $DD02 and $DD03 (56578 - 56579) for $DD00 and $DD01

Registers 4 - 7		**CIA #1**	**CIA #2**
Timer A	low-byte	$DC04	$DD04
Timer A	high-byte	$DC05	$DD05
Timer B	low-byte	$DC06	$DD06
Timer B	high-byte	$DC07	$DD07

CIA #1

These timers are used in updating the BASIC clock, in generating interrupts to read the keyboard and for other system functions.

CIA #2

User timer interrupts

Write   The 16 bit value written into the high high-byte, low-byte
         combination will cause an interrupt when the corresponding
         timer reaches that 16 bit value, if the correct enable bits
         are set.
Read   The 16 bit current value of the timer.

Registers 8 - 11	**CIA #1**	**CIA #2**
Time of Day clock : 1/10 seconds	$DC08	$DD08
Time of Day clock : seconds	$DC09	$DD09
Time of Day clock : minutes	$DC0A	$DD0A
Time of Day clock : bits 6 - 0 hours	$DC0B	$DD0B
bit 7 AM/PM		

CIA #1

For Basic and System clock

CIA #2

Write   Reset time — write to hours register stops the clock to allow
         you to set up all four time-of-day clock registers without
         losing accuracy, write to 1/10 seconds register restarts clock
         OR (depending on control register bit 7) set alarm function
         time.
Read   Reads time of day. When hours register is read, clock
         continues but present time will be READ on all registers
         until the 1/10 seconds registers is read.

Register 12	**CIA #1**	**CIA #2**
	$DC0C	$DD0C

Serial I/O Data Buffer

Register 13	**CIA #1**	**CIA #2**
	$DC0D	$DD0D

Write   bit 7   If set, written bits set to 1 will set
                  corresponding bit, written bits set to zero
                  will be unaffected.
                  If clear, written bits set to 0 will clear
                  corresponding bit, written bits set to zero will
                  be unaffected.

bits 4 - 0   Enable interrupts within CIA chip from
              stated areas.

Set/clear	—	—	Flag	Serial Port	Alarm	Timer B	Timer A

Read   bit 7   Interrupt has occurred.
        bits 4 - 0 Signals which of the following causes was
                    the source of the interrupt.

Interrupt	0	0	Flag	Serial Port	Alarm	Timer B	Timer A

CIA #1 — Flag — NMI Occurred.
CIA #2 — Flag — IRQ Occurred.

Register 14 - 15	**CIA #1**	**CIA #2**
Control Register A	$DC0E	$DD0E
Control Register B	$DC0F	$DD0F

Write   bit 0   1 - Start Timer
                  0 - Stop Timer
         bit 1   Timer overflow to appear in timer toggle
                  register 1. Timer A bit 6. Timer B bit 7.
         bit 2   Timer output mode to bit of register 1.
         bit 3   1 - One shot (count to zero then stop)
                  0 - Continuous (cycle)
         bit 4   1 - Load value into timer
                  0 - No action

Control Register A
         bit 5   1 - Timer A counts CNT signals
                  0 - Timer A counts system clock pulse
                  signals
         bit 6   1 - Serial port output
                  0 - Serial port input
         bit 7   1 - Clock on 50 Hz
                  0 - Clock on 60 Hz

Control Register B
         bits 5 - 6   00 - Count system clock pulse signals
                      01 - Count CNT signals
                      10 - Count Timer A underflow pulse signals
                      11 - Count Timer A underflow while CNT set

141

Appendix 9

Memory Usage Directory

List of low memory pointers, buffers and variables used by BASIC and the kernal.

Address (Hex)	Address (Decimal)	Description
0000	0	Chip directional register
0001 - 0002	1 - 2	Memory and tape control
0003 - 0004	3 - 4	Floating point - fixed point vector
0005 - 0006	5 - 6	Fixed point - floating point vector
0007	7	BASIC counter. Search character ':' or end of line
0008	8	Scan-quotes flag
0009	9	Column position of cursor on line
000A	10	Flag; 0 = LOAD, 1 = VERIFY
000B	11	BASIC input buffer point; subscript number
000C	12	Default DIM flag
000D	13	Variable type flag: FF = string, 00 = numeric
000E	14	Numeric type flag: 80 = integer, 00 = floating point
000F	15	DATA scan flag: LIST quote flag; memory flag
0010	16	Subscript flag; FNx flag
0011	17	Flag; 0 = INPUT, 152 = READ, 64 = GET
0012	18	ATN sign flag; comparison evaluation flag
0013	19	Current I/O prompt flag
0014 - 0015	20 - 21	Where BASIC stores integers used in calculations
0016	22	Temporary string stack pointer
0017 - 0018	23 - 24	Last temporary string vector
0019 - 0021	25 - 33	Stack for temporary string descriptions
0023 - 0025	34 - 37	Utility pointer area
0026 - 002A	38 - 42	Product area for multiplication
002B - 002C	43 - 44	Pointer to start of BASIC program
002D - 002E	45 - 46	Pointer to end of BASIC program; start of BASIC variables
002F - 0030	47 - 48	Pointer to end of variables; start of arrays

Address (Hex)	Address (Decimal)	Description
0033 - 0034	53 - 54	Pointer to end of string storage
0035 - 0036	55 - 56	Pointer to top of RAM available to BASIC
0037 - 0038	57 - 58	Current BASIC line number
0039 - 003A	59 - 60	Previous BASIC line number
003B - 003C	61 - 62	Pointer to BASIC statement (for CONT)
003D - 003E	63 - 64	Current DATA line number
003F - 0040	65 - 66	Pointer to current DATA item
0041 - 0042	67 - 68	Jump vector for INPUT statement
0043 - 0044	69 - 70	Current variable name
0045 - 0046	71 - 72	
0047 - 0048	71 - 71	Current variable address
0049 - 004A	73 - 74	Variable pointer for FOR/NEXT statement
004B - 004C	75 - 76	Y save; operator save; BASIC pointer save
004D	77	Comparison symbol
004E - 004F	78 - 79	Work area; function definition pointer
0050 - 0051	80 - 81	Work area; string descriptor pointer
0052	82	Length of string
0053	83	Garbage collect use
0054 - 0056	84 - 86	Jump vector for functions
0057 - 0060	87 - 96	Numeric work area
0061 - 0066	97 - 102	Floating point accumulator 1; Exponent, 4 byte Mantissa, Sign
0067	103	Series evaluation constant pointer
0068	104	Accumulator 1 overflow
0069 - 006E	105 - 110	Floating point accumulator 2
006F	111	Sign comparison - Acc 1 with Acc 2
0070	112	Acc 2 rounding
0071 - 0072	113 - 114	Cassette buffer length; series pointer
0073 - 008A	115 - 138	CHRGOT BASIC subroutine - gets next BASIC character
008B - 008F	139 - 143	RND storage and work area
0090	144	ST - status byte
0091	145	STOP and REVERSE flags; Keyswitch PIA
0092	146	Timing constant for tape
0093	147	Flag: 0 = LOAD, 1 = VERIFY
0094	148	Serial output: deferred character flag
0095	150	Tape EOT received
0097	151	Register save
0098	152	Number of OPEN files
0099	153	Current input device
009A	154	Current output (CMD) device
009B	155	Tape character parity
009C	156	Flag: byte received
009D	157	Output control flag: direct = 128; run = 0
009E	158	Tape pass 1 error log
009F	159	Tape pass 2 error log
00A0 - 00A2	160 - 162	Jifie clock - TI and TI$ use this

Address (Hex)	Address (Decimal)	Description
00A3	163	Serial bit count
00A4	164	Cycle count
00A5	165	Tape write bit count
00A6	166	Pointer to tape buffer
00A7	167	Tape write count; input bit storage
00A8	168	Tape write new byte; Read error; input bit count
00A9	169	Write start bit; Read bit error
00AA	170	Tape scan; count
00AB	171	Write read length; Read checksum; parity
00AC - 00AD	172 - 173	Pointer to tape buffer; scrolling
00AE - 00AF	174 - 175	Tape end addresses; end of program
00B0 - 00B1	176 - 177	Tape timing constants
00B2 - 00B3	178 - 179	Pointer to start of tape buffer
00B4	180	Tape timer; bit count
00B5	181	RS232 next bit to send
00B6	182	Read character error; next byte out
00B7	183	Number of characters in current file name
00B8	184	Current logical file number
00B9	185	Current secondary address
00BA	186	Current device number
00BB - 00BC	187 - 188	Pointer to current file name
00BD	189	Write shift byte; Read input character
00BE	190	Number of blocks remaining to Read/Write
008F	191	Serial word buffer
00C0	192	Tape motor interlock
00C1 - 00C2	193 - 194	I/O start addresses
00C3 - 00C4	195 - 196	KERNAL setup pointer
00C5	197	Current key pressed (see Appendix H)
00C6	198	Keyboard buffer counter
00C7	199	Flag: screen reverse - 1 is on, 0 is off
00C8	200	Pointer to end-of-line for input
00C9 - 00CA	201 - 202	Cursor log (row, column)
00CB	203	Current key pressed
00CC	204	Flag: cursor blink enable (0 is on)
00CD	205	Cursor blink delay
00CE	206	Character under cursor
00CF	207	Flag: cursor on/off
00D0	208	Input from screen/keyboard
00D1 - 00D2	209 - 210	Pointer to screen line on which cursor appears
00D3	211	Position of cursor on line
00D4	212	0 = direct cursor, else programmed
00D5	213	Screen line length, 21, 43, 65, 87
00D6	214	Current screen line number - To change cursor position, 201, 210, 211 and 214 must be changed
00D7	215	ASCII value of last character printed
00D8	216	Number of INSERTs outstanding

Address (Hex)	Address (Decimal)	Description
00D9 - 00F0	217 - 240	Screen line link table
00F1	241	Dummy screen line link
00F2	242	Screen row marker
00F3 - 00F4	243 - 244	Pointer to current location in colour memory
00F5 - 00F6	245 - 246	Pointer to keyscan table
00F7 - 00F8	247 - 248	Pointer to RS-232 receiver buffer start
00F9 - 00FA	249 - 250	Pointer to RS-232 transmitter buffer start
00FB - 00FE	251 - 254	Free zero-page locations
00FF	255	BASIC storage
0100 - 010A	256 - 266	Float - ASCII work area
0100 - 013E	256 - 318	Tape error log
0100 - 01FF	256 - 511	Processor stack area
0200 - 0258	512 - 600	BASIC input buffer
0259 - 0262	601 - 610	Logical file table for OPEN files
0263 - 026C	611 - 620	Device number table for OPEN files
026D - 0276	621 - 630	Secondary address table
0277 - 0280	631 - 640	Keyboard buffer
0281 - 0282	641 - 642	Pointer to start of memory for operating system
0283 - 0284	643 - 644	Pointer to end of memory for operating system
0285	645	Serial bus timeout flag
0286	646	Current colour code (for PRINTed character)
0287	647	Colour under cursor
0288	648	Screen memory page indicator
0289	649	Maximum length of keyboard buffer - must be less than 11
028A	650	Key autorepeat (0 = cursor controls, 255 = all)
028B	651	Pre-repeat delay
028C	652	Inter-repeat delay
028D	653	Keyboard flag for SHIFT, CTRL and C = keys. If SHIFT pressed, bit 0 is set, if CTRL, bit 1, if C = , bit 2
028E	654	Last shift pattern
028F - 0290	655 - 656	Pointer for keyboard table set-up
0291	657	Shift mode (0 = enabled, 128 = disabled)
0292	658	Auto scroll down flag (0 = on, else off)
0293	659	RS-232 control register
0294	660	RS-232 command register
0295 - 0296	661 - 662	Non-standard (bit time/2 - 100
0297	663	RS-232 status register
0298	664	Number of bits to send
0299 - 029A	665 - 666	Baud rate (full) bit time
029B	667	Pointer to RS-232 receiver buffer (end)
029C	668	Pointer to RS-232 receiver buffer (start)
029D	669	Pointer to RS-232 transmit buffer (start)
029E	670	Pointer to RS-232 transmit buffer (end)
029F - 02A0	671 - 672	Holds IRQ during tape operations
02A1	673	CIA 2 (NMI) Interrupt control

Address (Hex)	Address (Decimal)	Description
02A2	674	CIA 1 Timer A control log
02A3	675	CIA 1 Interrupt log
02A4	676	CIA 1 Timer A enable flag
02A5	677	Screen row marker
02A6	678	PAL/NISC flag, 0 = NTSC, 1 = PAL
02A7 - 02FF	679 - 767	UNUSED
0300 - 0301	768 - 769	Error message link
0302 - 0303	770 - 771	Basic warm start link
0304 - 0305	772 - 773	Tokenization routine link
0306 - 0307	774 - 775	Print tokens link
0308 - 0309	776 - 777	Start new BASIC code link
030A - 030B	778 - 779	Get arithmetic element link
030C	780	Temporary storage of A during SYS
030D	781	Temporary storage of X during SYS
030E	782	Temporary storage of Y during SYS
030F	783	Temporary storage of P during SYS
0310 - 0311	784 - 785	USR function jump
0314 - 0315	788 - 789	Hardware interrupt vector (EA31)
0316 - 0317	790 - 791	Break (BRK) interrupt vector (FE66)
0318 - 0319	792 - 793	NMI interrupt vector (FE47)
031A - 031B	794 - 795	OPEN vector (F34A)
031C - 031D	796 - 797	CLOSE vector (F291)
031E - 031F	798 - 799	Set input device vector (F20E)
0320 - 0321	800 - 801	Set output device vector (F250)
0322 - 0323	802 - 803	Restore I/O vector (F333)
0324 - 0325	804 - 805	Input vector (F157)
0326 - 0327	806 - 807	Output vector (F1CA)
0328 - 0329	808 - 809	Test STOP-key vector (F6ED)
032A - 032B	810 - 811	GET vector (F13E)
032C - 032D	812 - 813	Close all files vector (F32F)
032E - 032F	814 - 815	User vector (FE66)
0330 - 0331	816 - 817	Load-from-device vector (F4A5)
0332 - 0333	818 - 819	Save to device vector (F5ED)
0334 - 033B	820 - 827	UNUSED
033C - 03FB	828 - 1019	Cassette buffer - useful for holding machine code when no files are being used
03FC - 03FF	1020 - 1023	UNUSED

Appendix 10

Operating System Routines

We have presented here a list of routines in the ROM and their starting address. Some of them are part of BASIC and some are part of the Kernal. For those which are most commonly used we have supplied more detailed descriptions about their function and their usage. To use these subroutines to set up required variables, call any preparatory subroutines, call the subroutine and then check for any errors which may have occurred.

Name, Purpose

Address : in hex

Communication registers: registers used to pass information to and from the KERNAL subroutine.

Preparatory routines: these routines must be called prior to the subroutine in question.

Possible errors: if an error occurs, when the subroutine returns the carry flag will be set, and the error code will be in the accumulator.

Stack: number of bytes of stack used by the routine.

Registers used: a list of all registers used by the KERNAL routine.

1. Name: ACPTR
   Purpose: Get data from serial bus
   Address: $FFA5
   Communication registers: A; data returned in accumulator
   Prep. routines: TALK, TKSA
   Possible errors: see READST
   Stack: 13
   Registers used: X, A

2. Name: CHKIN
   Purpose: Open a channel for input
   Address: $FFC6
   Communication registers: X; load X with number of logical file to be used
   Prep routines: OPEN
   Possible errors: 3, 5, 6
   Stack: 0
   Registers used: A, X

3. Name: CHKOUT
   Purpose: Open a channel for output
   Address: $FFC9
   Communication registers: X; load X with logical file number to be used
   Prep. routines: OPEN
   Possible errors: 3, 5, 7
   Stack: 0
   Registers used: A, X

4. Name: CHRIN
   Purpose: Get a character from input channel
   Address: $FFCF
   Communication registers: A; data byte returned in A
   Prep. routines: OPEN, CHKIN (unless device is keyboard)
   Possible errors: see READST
   Stack: 0
   Registers used: A, X

5. Name: CHROUT
   Purpose: Output a character
   Address: $FFD2
   Communication registers: A; load byte to be output in A
   Prep. routines: OPEN, CHKOUT (unless device is screen)
   Possible errors: see READST
   Stack: 0
   Registers used: A

6. Name: CIOUT
   Purpose: Transmit a byte over the serial bus
   Address: $FFA8
   Communication registers: A; load byte to be output in A
   Prep. routines: LISTEN, (SECOND if device needs secondary address)
   Possible errors: see READST
   Stack: 0
   Registers used: A

7. Name: CLALL
   Purpose: Close all files
   Address: $FFE7
   Communication registers: none
   Prep. routines: none
   Possible errors: none
   Stack: 11
   Registers used: A, X

8. Name: CLOSE
   Purpose: Close a logical file
   Address: $FFC3

150

Communication registers: A; load A with logical file number to be closed
Prep. routines: none
Possible errors: none
Stack: 0
Registers used: A, X

9. Name: CLRCHIN
   Purpose: Clear I/O channels
   Address: $FFCC
   Communication registers: none
   Prep. routines: none
   Possible errors: none
   Stack: 9
   Registers used: A, X

10. Name: GETIN
    Purpose: Get a character from keyboard buffer
    Address: $FFE4
    Communication registers: A; character code returned in A
    Prep. routines: none
    Possible errors: none
    Stack: 0
    Registers used: A, X

11. Name: IOBASE
    Purpose: Define I/O memory page
    Address: $FFF3
    Communication registers: X, Y; respectively low and high address bytes of memory section where memory mapped I/O devices are located are returned in X, Y
    Prep. routines: none
    Possible errors: none
    Stack: Two registers used: X, Y

12. Name: LISTEN
    Purpose: Command a device on the serial bus to receive data
    Address: $FFB1
    Communication registers: A; load A with number 4-1, 3 indicating device.
    Prep. routines: none
    Possible errors: see READST
    Stack: 0
    Registers used: A

13. Name: LOAD
    Purpose: Load RAM from device, or verify
    Address: $FFD5
    Communication registers: A; set to 0 for load, 1 for verify. X, Y; low and high bytes of starting address of load

151

Prep. routines: SETLFS, SETNAM
Possible errors: 0, 4, 5, 8, 9
Stack: 0
Registers used: A, X, Y

14. Name: MEMBOT

Purpose: Set or read the address of the bottom of RAM

Address: $FF9C

Communication registers: Carry flag; 1 to read, 0 to set bottom of memory. X, Y; low and high bytes of address. If carry is set, the address will be returned in X, Y. If carry clear, address in X, Y will be transferred to pointer to bottom of RAM

Prep. routines: none

Possible errors: none

Stack: 0

Registers used: X, Y, P

15. Name: MEMTOP

Purpose: Set or read the address on top of RAM

Address: $FF99

Communication registers: Carry, X, Y; as for MEMBOT

Prep. routines: none

Possible errors: none

Stack: 2

Registers used: X, Y, Carry

16. Name: OPEN

Purpose: Open a logical file

Address: $FFC0

Communication registers: none

Prep. routines: SETLFS, SETNAM

Possible errors: 1, 2, 4, 5, 6

Stack: 0

Registers used: A, X, Y

17. Name: PLOT

Purpose: Set cursor location or read cursor location

Address: $FFF0

Communication registers: Carry: 1 for set cursor location 0 for read cursor location. X; column number (0 - 21) returned to or loaded from. Y; row number (0 - 22) returned to or loaded from.

Prep. routines: none

Possible errors: none

Stack: 2

Registers used: Carry, X, Y

18. Name: RDTIM

Purpose: Read system clock-3 byte value

Address: $FFDE

Communication registers: A; most significant byte returned. X; next most significant byte returned. Y; lease significant byte returned.
Prep. routines: none
Possible errors: none
Stack: 2
Registers used: A, X, Y

19. Name: READST
Purpose: read status word and setup errors.
Address: $FFB7
Communication registers: A; error code returned in A. See discussion of ST in BASIC section for codes and meanings
Prep. routines: none
Possible errors: none
Stack: 2
Registers used: A

20. Name: RESTOR
Purpose: Restore default system and interrupt vectors
Address: $FF8A
Communication registers: none
Prep. routines: none
Possible errors: none
Stack: 2
Registers used: A, X, Y

21. Name: SAVE
Purpose: Save memory to a device
Address: $FFD8
Communication registers: A; load with zero-page address. This address and the next byte contain the address of the start of memory to be saved. X, Y; low and high bytes of end address of memory to be saved.
Prep. routines: SETLFS, SETNAM (SETNAM not needed if a nameless save to Datasette is desired)
Possible errors: 5, 8, 9
Stack: 0
Registers used: A, X, Y

22. Name: SCNKEY
Purpose: Scan the keyboard, put value in keyboard queue
Address: $FF9F
Communication registers: none
Prep. routines: none
Possible errors: none
Stack: 0
Registers used: A, X, Y

23. Name: SCREEN
    Purpose: Return number of screen rows and columns
    Address: $FFED
    Communication registers: X; number of columns returned in X. Y; number of rows returned in Y
    Prep. routines: none
    Possible errors: none
    Stack: 2
    Registers used: X, Y

24. Name: SECOND
    Purpose: Send secondary address for LISTEN
    Address: $FF93
    Communication registers: A; load with secondary address to be sent
    Prep. routines: LISTEN
    Possible errors: see READST
    Stack: 0
    Registers used: A

25. Name: SETLFS
    Purpose: Set up a logical file number, device and secondary addresses
    Address: $FFBA
    Communication registers: A; load logical file number into A. X; device number. Y; command (secondary address)
    Prep. routines: none
    Possible errors: none
    Stack: 2
    Registers used: A, X, Y

26. Name: SETNAM
    Purpose: Set up file name
    Address: $FFBD
    Communication registers: A; load length of file name into A. X,Y; low, high bytes of address of start of memory where file name is stored
    Prep. routines: none
    Possible errors: none
    Stack: 0
    Registers used: A, X, Y

27. Name: SETTIM
    Purpose: Set the system clock-3 byte value
    Address: $FFDB
    Communication registers: A; most significant byte. X; next most significant byte. Y; least significant byte
    Prep. routines: none

Possible errors: none
Stack: 2
Registers used: A, X, Y

28. Name: STOP
    Purpose: Check if stop key pressed
    Address: $FFE1
    Communication registers: zero flag; set if STOP key pressed
    Prep. routines: none
    Possible errors: none
    Stack: 0
    Registers used: zero flag, A, X

29. Name: TALK
    Purpose: Command a device on the serial bus to TALK
    Address: $FFB4
    Communication registers: A; load device number into A
    Prep. routines: none
    Possible errors: see READST
    Stack: 0
    Registers used: A

30. Name: TKSA
    Purpose: send a secondary address to a device commanded to
      TALK
    Address: $FF96
    Communication registers: A; load secondary address into A
    Prep. routines: TALK
    Possible errors: see READST
    Stack: 0
    Registers used: A

31. Name: UNLSN
    Purpose: Command all devices on the serial bus to stop receiving
      data
    Address: $FFAE
    Communication registers: none
    Possible errors: see READST
    Stack: 0
    Registers used: A

32. Name: UNTLK
    Purpose: Send an UNTALK command to all devices on serial bus
    Address: $FFAB
    Communication registers: none
    Prep. routines: none
    Possible errors: see READST
    Stack: 0
    Registers used: A

33. Name: VECTOR
    Purpose: Set or read system RAM vectors
    Address: $FF8D
    Communication registers: X, Y; address of list of system RAM
        vectors. Carry flag; if set, the RAM vectors are read into the list
        pointed to by X, Y and if clear, the contents of the list pointed to by
        X, Y are read into the RAM vectors.
    Prep. routines: none
    Possible errors: none
    Stack: 2
    Registers used: Carry flag, X, Y

Error Codes

Value	Meaning
0	Routine terminated by STOP key
1	Too many open files
2	File already open
3	File not open
4	File not found
5	Device not present
6	File is not an input file
7	File is not an output file
8	File name is missing
9	Illegal device number

Kernal ROM Routines

Address (Hex)	Address (Decimal)	Function of Routine
E097	57495	RND
E12A	57642	SYS
E156	57686	SAVE
E165 *< 168*	57701	LOAD
E1BE	57790	OPEN
E1C7	57799	CLOSE
E1D4	57812	Parameters for LOAD/SAVE
E20E	57870	Check for comma
E219	57881	Parameters for OPEN/CLOSE
E264	57956	COS
E26B	57963	SIN
E2B4	58036	TAN
E30E	58126	ATN
E37B	58235	Warm start
E394	58260	Initialize
E3A2	58274	CHRGET for zero page
E3BF	58292	Initialize BASIC
E453	58451	Initialize vectors
E45F	58463	Power-up message
E500	58624	Get I/O address
E505	58629	Get screen size
E50A	58634	Put/get row/column
E518	58648	Initialize I/O
E544	58692	Clear screen
E566	58726	Home cursor
E56C	58732	Set screen pointers
E5A0	58784	Set I/O defaults
E5B4	58804	Input from keyboard
E632	58930	Input from screen
E684	59012	Quote test
E691	59025	Setup screen print
E6B6	59062	Advance cursor
E6ED	59117	Retreat cursor
E701	59137	Previous line
E716	59158	Output to screen
E87C	59516	Go to next line
E891	59537	<return> key
E8CB	59592	Set colour code
E8EA	59626	Scroll screen
E965	59749	Open space on screen
E9C8	59848	Move a screen line
E9F0	59888	Interrupt
EA87	60039	Read keyboard
EB79	60281	Keyboard select vectors
EB81	60289	Keyboard 1 – unshifted

Address (Hex)	Address (Decimal)	Function of Routine
EBC2	60354	Keyboard 2 – shifted
EC03	60419	Keyboard 3 – 'comm'
EC44	60484	Graphics/text control
EC4F	60495	Set graphics/text mode
EC78	60536	Keyboard 4
ECB9	60601	Video chip setup
ECF9	60665	Screen in address low
ED0B	60683	Send 'talk'
ED11	60689	Send 'listen'
ED40	60736	Send to serial bus
EDB2	60850	Serial timeout
EDEF	60911	Send 'untalk'
EE03	60931	Send 'unlisten'
EE13	60947	Receive from serial bus
EE85	61061	Serial clock on
EE8E	61070	Serial clock off
EE97	61079	Serial output '1'
EEA0	61088	Serial output '0'
EEA9	61097	Get serial in
EEBB	61115	RS-232 send
EF06	61190	Send new RS-232 byte
EF3B	61243	Disable timer
EF4A	61258	Compute bit count
EF59	61273	RS-232 receive
EF7E	61310	Setup to receive
EFC4	61380	Receive parity error
EFCC	61388	Receive overflow
EFCF	61391	Receive break
EFD2	61394	Framing error
F017	61463	Send to RS-232 buffer
F04D	61517	Input from RS-232
F0A4	61604	Check serial bus idle
F13E	61758	Get . .
F157	61783	Input
F199	61849	Get . . tape/serial/RS-232
F1CA	61898	Output . .
F20E	61966	Set input device
F250	62032	Set output device
F291	62097	Close file
F30F	62223	Find file
F31F	62239	Set file values
F32F	62255	Abort all files
F333	62259	Restore default I/O
F34A	62282	Open file
F409	62473	Open RS-232
F49E	62622	Load program
F5AF	62895	'searching'

Address (Hex)	Address (Decimal)	Function of Routine
F5C1	62913	Print filename
F5D2	62930	'loading/verifying'
F5DD	62941	Save program
F68F	63119	Print 'saving'
F69B	63131	Bump clock
F6BC	63164	Log PIA key reading
F6DD	63197	Get time
F6E4	63204	Set time
F6ED	63213	Check stop key
F6FB	63227	Output error messages
F72C	63276	Find any tape header
F76A	63338	Write tape header
F7D0	63440	Get buffer address
F7D7	63447	Set buffer start/end pointers
F817	63511	'press play'
F82E	63534	Check tape status
F838	63544	'press record'
F841	63553	Start tape read
F864	63588	Start tape write
F8D0	63696	Check tape stop
F8E2	63714	Set read timing
F92C	63788	Read tape bits
FA60	64096	Store tape chars.
FB8E	64398	Reset pointer
FBC8	64456	Write data to tape
FBCD	64461	IRQ entry point
FC57	64599	Write tape leader
FC93	64659	Restore normal IRQ
FCB8	64696	Set IRQ vector
FCCA	64714	Kill tape motor
FCD1	64721	Check r/w pointer
FCDB	64731	Bump r/w pointer
FCE2	64738	Power reset entry
FD15	64789	Kernal reset
FD1A	64794	Kernal move
FD30	64816	Vectors
FD50	64848	Initialize system consts.
FD9B	64923	IRQ vectors
FDA3	64931	Initialize I/O
FDDD	64989	Enable timer
FDF9	65017	Save filename data
FE00	65024	Save file details
FE07	65031	Get status
FE18	65048	Flag status
FE1C	65052	Set status
FE21	65057	Set timeout
FE25	65061	Read/set top of memory
FE27	65063	Read top of memory

FE2D	65069	Set top of memory
FE34	65076	Read/set bottom of memory
FE43	65091	NMI entry
FE66	65126	Warm start
FEB6	65206	Reset IRQ & exit
FEBC	65212	Interrupt exit
FF43	65347	Fake IRQ
FF48	65352	IRQ entry
FF81	65409	Jump table
FFF6	65526	Hardware vectors

'BASIC' ROM Routines

Address (Hex)	Address (Decimal)	Function of Routine
A000	40960	ROM control vectors
A00C	40972	Keyword Execution vectors
A052	41042	Function vectors
A080	41088	Operator vectors
A09E	41118	Keywords
A19E	41374	Error messages
A328	41768	Error message vectors
A35B	41816	Miscellaneous messages
A389	41865	Scan stack for FOR/GOSUB
A3B8	41912	Move memory
A3FB	41979	Check stack depth
A408	41992	Check memory length
A435	42037	'out of memory'
A437	42039	Error
A469	42089	BREAK
A474	42100	'ready'
A480	42112	Ready for BASIC
A49C	42140	Handle new line
A533	42291	Re-chain lines
A560	42336	Receive input line
A579	42361	Crunch tokens
A613	42515	Find BASIC line
A642	42562	NEW
A65E	42590	CLR
A68E	42638	Back up text pointer
A69C	42652	LIST
A742	42818	FOR
A7ED	42989	Execute statement
A81D	43037	RESTORE
A82C	43052	Break
A82F	43055	STOP
A831	43057	END
A857	43095	CONT
A871	43121	RUN

Address (Hex)	Address (Decimal)	Function of Routine
A883	43139	GOSUB
A8A0	43168	GOTO
A8D2	43218	RETURN
A8F8	43256	DATA
A906	43270	Scan for next statement
A928	43304	IF
A93B	43323	REM
A94B	43339	ON
A96B	43371	Get fixed point number
A9A5	43429	LET
AA80	43648	PRINT#
AA86	43654	CMD
AAA0	43680	PRINT
AB1E	43806	Print string from (y.a)
AB3B	43835	Print format character
AB4D	43853	Bad input routine
AB7B	43899	GET
ABA5	43941	INPUT#
ABBF	43967	INPUT
ABF9	44025	Prompt & input
AC06	44038	READ
ACFC	44284	Input error messages
AD1E	44318	NEXT
AD78	44408	Type match check
AD9E	44446	Evaluate expression
AEA8	44712	Constant — pi
AEF1	44785	Calculate brackets
AEF7	44791	')'
AEFF	44799	Comma
AF08	44808	Syntax error
AF14	44820	Check range
AF28	44840	Search for variable
AFA7	44967	Setup FN
AFE9	45033	OR
AFF0	45040	AND
B016	45078	Compare
B081	45185	DIM
B08B	45195	Locate variable
B113	45331	Check alphabetic
B11D	45341	Create variable
B194	45460	Array pointer subroutine
B1A5	45477	Value 32768
B1B2	45490	Float-fixed
B1D1	45521	Set up array
B248	45640	'bad subscript'
B24D	45645	'illegal quantity'
B34C	45900	Compute array size

Address (Hex)	Address (Decimal)	Function of Routine
B37D	45949	Perform [FRE]
B391	45969	Fix-float
B39E	45982	Perform [POS]
B3A6	45990	Check direct
B3B3	46003	Perform [DEF]
B3E1	46049	Check fn syntax
B3F4	46068	Perform [FN]
B465	46181	Perform [STR$]
B475	46197	Calculate string vector
B487	46215	Set up string
B4F4	46324	Make room for string
B526	46374	Garbage collection
B5BD	46525	Check salvageability
B606	46598	Collect string
B63D	46653	Concatenate
B67A	46714	Build string to memory
B6A3	46755	Discard unwanted string
B6DB	46811	Clean descriptor stack
B6EC	46828	Perform [CHR$]
B700	46848	Perform [LEFT$]
B72C	46892	Perform [RIGHT$]
B737	46903	Perform [MID$]
B761	46945	Pull string parameters
B77C	46972	Perform [LEN]
B782	46978	Exit string-mode
B78B	46987	Perform [ASC]
B79B	47003	Input byte parameter
B7AD	47021	Perform [VAL]
B7EB	47083	Parameters for POKE/WAIT
B7F7	47095	Float-fixed
B80D	47117	Perform [PEEK]
B824	47140	Perform [POKE]
B82D	46125	Perform [WAIT]
B849	47177	Add 0.5
B850	47184	Subtract − from
B853	47187	Perform [subtract]
B86A	47210	Perform [add]
B947	47431	Complement FAC#1
B97E	47486	'overflow'
B983	47491	Multiply by zero byte
B9EA	47594	Perform [LOG]
BA2B	47659	Multiply
BA59	47705	Multiply-a-bit
BA8C	47756	Memory to FAC#2
BAB7	47799	Adjust FAC#1/#2
BAD4	47828	Underflow/overflow
BAE2	47842	Multiply by 10

162

Address (Hex)	Address (Decimal)	Function of Routine
BAF9	47865	+ 10 in floating pt.
BAFE	47870	Divide by 10
BB12	47890	Divide
BBA2	48034	Memory to FAC#1
BBC7	48071	FAC#1 to memory
BBFC	48124	FAC#2 to FAC#1
BC0C	48140	FAC#1 to FAC#2
BC1B	48155	Round FAC#1
BC2B	48171	Get sign
BC39	48185	SGN
BC58	48216	ABS
BC5B	48219	Compare FAC#1 to mem.
BC9B	48283	Float-fixed
BCCC	48332	int
BCF3	48371	String to FAC(VAL)
BD7E	48510	Get ASCII digit
BDC2	48578	Print
BDCD	48589	Print line number
BDDD	48605	Float to ASCII
BF16	48918	Decimal constants
BF3A	48954	TI constants
BF71	49009	SQR
BF7B	49019	Power
BFB4	49076	Negative
BFED	49133	EXP

163

Appendix 11

Table of Screen Codes

This is a list of the characters that will be displayed when the number in the value column is placed in screen memory while in normal text mode.

Set 1 and Set 2 refer to the two different character sets available. The same value in memory may display a different character, depending on which character set is being displayed. To switch between the two character sets you can either press the shift and Commodore keys together, or you can change the value of the character memory pointer byte at $D018 (53272) between its normal value $15 (21) upper case and graphics (set 1), and $17 (23) upper and lower case (set 2).

NOTE: where only one symbol appears for a particular value, that symbol is displayed by both character sets.

SCREEN CODES

Value	Set 1	Set 2	Value	Set1	Set 2	Value	Set 1	Set 2	Value	Set 1	Set 2
0	@		32	SPACE		64	[graphic]		96	SPACE	
1	A	a	33	!		65	♠	A	97	[graphic]	
2	B	b	34	"		66	[graphic]	B	98	[graphic]	
3	C	c	35	#		67	[graphic]	C	99	[graphic]	
4	D	d	36	$		68	[graphic]	D	100	[graphic]	
5	E	e	37	%		69	[graphic]	E	101	[graphic]	
6	F	f	38	&		70	[graphic]	F	102	[graphic]	
7	G	g	39	'		71	[graphic]	G	103	[graphic]	
8	H	h	40	(		72	[graphic]	H	104	[graphic]	
9	I	i	41	)		73	[graphic]	I	105	[graphic]	[graphic]
10	J	j	42	*		74	[graphic]	J	106	[graphic]	
11	K	k	43	+		75	[graphic]	K	107	[graphic]	
12	L	l	44	,		76	[graphic]	L	108	[graphic]	
13	M	m	45	–		77	[graphic]	M	109	[graphic]	
14	N	n	46	.		78	[graphic]	N	110	[graphic]	
15	O	o	47	/		79	[graphic]	O	111	[graphic]	
16	P	p	48	0		80	[graphic]	P	112	[graphic]	
17	Q	q	49	1		81	[graphic]	Q	113	[graphic]	
18	R	r	50	2		82	[graphic]	R	114	[graphic]	
19	S	s	51	3		83	♥	S	115	[graphic]	
20	T	t	52	4		84	[graphic]	T	116	[graphic]	
21	U	u	53	5		85	[graphic]	U	117	[graphic]	
22	V	v	54	6		86	⊠	V	118	[graphic]	
23	W	w	55	7		87	◯	W	119	[graphic]	
24	X	x	56	8		88	♣	X	120	[graphic]	
25	Y	y	57	9		89	[graphic]	Y	121	[graphic]	
26	Z	z	58	:		90	♦	Z	122	[graphic]	[graphic]
27	[		59	;		91	[graphic]		123	[graphic]	
28	£		60	<		92	[graphic]		124	[graphic]	
29	]		61	=		93	[graphic]		125	[graphic]	
30	↑		62	>		94	[graphic]	[graphic]	126	[graphic]	
31	←		63	?		95	[graphic]	[graphic]	127	[graphic]	

Appendix 12

Current Key Pressed

Location 197 stores a coded value of the current key pressed. If more than one key is pressed the higher value is stored.

Value	Key	Value	Key
0	DEL	35	0
1	RETURN	36	M
2	CRSR→	37	K
3	F7	38	O
4	F1	39	N
5	F3	40	+
6	F5	41	P
7	CRSR ↓	42	L
8	3	43	−
9	W	44	.
10	A	45	:
11	4	46	@
12	Z	47	,
13	S	48	£
14	E	49	.
15	NONE	50	;
16	5	51	CLEAR
17	R	52	NONE
18	D	53	=
19	6	54	↑
20	C	55	/
21	F	56	1
22	T	57	←
23	X	58	NONE
24	7	59	2
25	Y	60	SPACE
26	G	61	NONE
27	8	62	Q
28	B	63	NONE
29	H		
30	U		
31	V		
32	9		
33	I		
34	J		

Appendix 13

```
0       REM
100     REM *********** ALPA ***********
110     REM *     P.ROSHAM, 12/4/1984    *
111     REM *         AND DANNY DAVIS    *
112     REM *                            *
115     REM *      ASSEMBLY LANGUAGE     *
116     REM *       PROGRAMMING AID      *
118     REM *                            *
120     REM ****************************
150     GOTO 9000
1000    REM
1010    REM PROCESS LINE
1020    REM
1030    F=0:FM=0:ER=0
1040    FOR J=P1 TO P2
1050    IF C$(J,1)=" ▲ ▲ " THEN 1110
1053    CO$=C$(J,1):IFC$(J,2)<>" ▲ ▲ "THEN CO$=CO$+C$(J,2)
1054    IFC$(J,3)<>" ▲ ▲ "THEN CO$=CO$+C$(J,3)
1055    GOSUB30000
1056    IF ER>0 THEN 1110
1061    IF J<100 THENPRINT" ▲ ";
1062    IF J<10 THENPRINT" ▲ ";
1069    PRINT J;": ▲ ";
1070    IF LEFT$(C$(J,2),1)="L" THEN 1075
1071    GOTO 1080
1075    PRINTC$(J,1)+" ▲ "+C$(J,2)+C$(J,3);" ▲ ";:GOTO1090
1080    PRINTC$(J,1);" ▲ ";C$(J,2);" ▲ ";C$(J,3);
1090    F=F+1
1095    PRINTSPC(8);DI$
1100    IF F=22 THEN GOTO 1120
1110    NEXT J
1120    RETURN
2000    REM
2010    REM MAIN ROUTINE
2020    A$="":INPUT"COMMAND ▲ OR ▲ LINE(###) ▲ : ▲ ";A$
2040    IF LEFT$(A$,1)>"9" GOTO3000
2042    PRINT" ▢ ";:FOR I=1TO 36:PRINT" ▲ ";:NEXTI:PRINTCHR$(13);"
        ▢ ";
2045    IF LEFT$(A$,1)<"0"GOTO 2020
2050    K$="":FOR K=1TO 4
2060    IF MID$(A$,K,1)=" ▲ " GOTO 2090
2065    IF MID$(A$,K,1)="" THEN A$=" ▲ ▲ ▲ ▲ ▲ ▲ ▲ ▲ ":J
        =VAL(K$):N=J:GOTO 2170
2067    IF MID$(A$,K,1)>"9"ORMID$(A$,K,1)<"0" THEN PRINT"INVALID
        ▲ LINE ▲ #":GOTO 2020
2070    K$=K$+MID$(A$,K,1)
2080    NEXT K
```

```
2090   IF K=5 OR VAL(K$)=ZE OR VAL(K$)>LN GOTO 2020
2100   J=VAL(K$):N=J
2110   A$=RIGHT$(A$,(LEN(A$)-K))
2120   LET K$=""
2130   FORK=1 TO LEN(A$)
2140   IF MID$(A$,K,1)<>" " THENK$=K$+MID$(A$,K,1)
2150   NEXT K

2160   A$=K$
2162   IF LEFT$(A$,1)="L"THEN GOTO 2020
2170   FORI=1 TO 5 STEP 2
2180   K=INT(I/2+1)
2190   C$(J,K)=MID$(A$,I,2)
2195   C$(J,K)=LEFT$(C$(J,K)+"   ",2)
2200   NEXTI
2210   IF C$(N,OE)="   "THEN2250
2220   IF N<TP THENTP=N
2230   IF N>BPTHENBP=N
2240   GOTO2320
2250   IFN<>BP GOTO2280
2260   IF BP=1 OR C$(BP,1)<>"   "GOTO2320
2270   BP=BP-OE:GOTO2260
2280   IF N<>TP GOTO2320
2290   IF C$(TP,OE)<>"   "THENGOTO2320
2300   IF TP<>BP AND TP<>LN THENTP=TP+OE:GOTO2290
2310   TP=OE
2320   PP=N
2330   IF N<TP THEN PP=TP:GOTO2380
2340   NU=ZE
2350   IF PP=TP OR NU=0 THENGOTO2380
2360   IF C$(PP,OE)<>"   " THENNU=NU+OE
2370   PP=PP-OE:GOTO2350
2380   P1=PP:P2=PP
2385   IF C$(N,1)="   " THEN 2020
2390   GOSUB 1000
2391   IF ER=1 THEN PRINT"ILLEGAL  OP-CODE"
2392   IF ER=2 THEN PRINT"INVALID  OP-CODE"
2393   IF ER=3 THEN PRINT"INVALID  LENGTH  OPERAND"
2394   IF ER=4 THEN PRINT"ILLEGAL  OPERAND"
2400   GOTO 2020
2590   REM**********WATCH/NOWATCH
2600   INPUT"WATCH  WHAT  ADDRESS  :  ";QZ$:XQ$=RIGHT$(("0000
       "+QZ$),4)
2610   GOSUB 15000:IF ER=1 THEN 2600
2620   WQ=XQ:WQ$=XQ$:GOTO2020
2630   IF WA<>1 THEN2640
2635   PRINT"ADDRESS  ";WQ$;"=   (BEFORE)  $";:ET=PEEK(WQ):
       GOSUB 40000
2636   PRINTRIGHT$(HB$,2)
2640   IF PEEK(R)=0 THEN PRINT "NO  PROGRAM  IN  MEMORY":PRINT
       :GOTO 2645
2641   SYS R
2645   IF WA<>1 THEN2660
2650   PRINT"ADDRESS  ";WQ$;"=   (AFTER  )  $";:ET=PEEK(WQ)
       :GOSUB 40000
2655   PRINTRIGHT$(HB$,2)
2660   GOTO2020
2700   REM *********DUMP MEMORY
2710   DC$="0000"
```

170

```
2720    INPUT"DUMP _ FROM _ WHAT _ ADDRESS _ ";DM$
2730    XQ$=RIGHT$((DC$+DM$),4):GOSUB15000:IF ER=1 THEN 2720
2740    DM=XQ
2750    PRINT" ▙ DUMPING _ FROM _ ADDRESS _ $";XQ$
2755    G=DM
2760    FOR MM=G TO(G+176)STEP 8:F$=""
2765    ET=MM:GOSUB40000:PRINTHB$;" _ : _ ";
2770    FOR MW=0TO7:MQ(MW)=PEEK(MM+MW)
2775    A=MQ(MW):IF A<32 OR A>127 OR A>159 THEN F$=F$+CHR$(32):
        GOTO2780
2776    F$=F$+CHR$(A)
2780    H=INT(MQ(MW)/16):L=MQ(MW)-16*H
2785    PRINTMID$(D$,H+1,1)+MID$(D$,L+1,1);
2789    NEXT MW:PRINT SPC(8);F$
2790    NEXT MM
2795    GET K$:IF K$="" THEN 2795
2800    IF K$<>"M" THEN G=MM:GOTO2760
2810    GOTO 2020
3000    REM
3005    IF A$="" GOTO 2020
3010    REM ****** COMMANDS ******
3020    K$=LEFT$(A$,TW)
3030    IF K$="EN" THEN 5000
3040    IF K$="QU" THEN STOP
3044    IF K$="WA" THEN WA=1:GOTO 2600
3046    IF K$="NW" THEN WA=0: GOTO 2020
3050    IF K$="LI" THEN 4000
3060    IF K$="LO" THEN 7000
3070    IF K$="ME" THEN 6000
3080    IF K$="NE" THEN RUN
3090    IF K$="RU" THEN GOTO 2630
3100    IF K$="SA" THEN 8000
3110    IF K$="CH" THEN 9150
3115    IF K$="DU" THEN 2700
3119    PRINT"INVALID _ COMMAND _ "
3120    GOTO2000
4000    REM
4010    REM **** LIST ROUNTINE ******
4020    P1=TP:P2=BP
4025    IFLEN(A$)<5 THEN 4040
4030    N1=ASC(MID$(A$,6,1))
4040    IF LEN(A$)>FR AND N1>47 AND N1<58 THEN P1=VAL(MID$(A$,5,3)
        )
4045    PRINT " ▙ "
4050    GOSUB 1000
4060    GOTO2020
5000    REM
5010    REM DUNPROUTINE *******
5020    G=R:PRINT"ENTERING _ AT _ ADDRESS _ $";:ET=G:GOSUB40000:
        PRINTHB$
5040    FOR J=TP TO BP
5050    IF C$(J,OE)=" _ "THENGOTO5470
5060    IF MID$(C$(J,TW),1,1)<>"L" THEN5380
5070    POKE G,ZE:POKEG+OE,ZE:POKE G+TW,ZE:POKE G+TR,ZE
5080    J1=VAL(MID$(C$(J,TW),TW,1)+C$(J,TR))
5090    IFLEFT$(C$(J,2),1)="L"THENPRINTJ;" _ : _ ";C$(J,1)+" _ "+C
        $(J,2)+C$(J,3):GOTO5100
5095    PRINTJ;" _ : _ ";C$(J,1);" _ ";C$(J,2);C$(J,3)
5100    IF J1<ZE OR J1>LN THEN5460
```

171

```
5110    JJ$=C$(J,1):GOSUB 20000:CJ=JJ
5120    IFLEFT$(C$(J,2),1)<>"L" THEN 5125
5121    PRINTJ1;" ▲ : ▲ ";C$(J1,1)+" ▲ "+C$(J1,2)+C$(J1,3):GOTO513
        0
5125    PRINTJ1;" ▲ : ▲ ";C$(J1,1);" ▲ ";C$(J1,2);" ▲ ";C$(J1,3)
5130    IF ABS(CJ)<> OE THENGOTO5460
5140    DD=(J1<J)-(J1>J)
5150    JA=G:DP=ZE
5160    IF J1=J THENGOTO5270
5170    CL=J+DD
5180    N1=ZE:IF C$(CL,OE)=" ▲ ▲ "THENGOTO5220
5190    IF LEFT$(C$(CL,2),1)="L" GOTO5200
5192    N1=OE-(C$(CL,TW)<>" ▲ ▲ ")-(C$(CL,TR)<>" ▲ ▲ "):GOTO5220
5200    JJ$=C$(CL,1):GOSUB 20000:TJ=JJ
5210    N1=((TJ=OE)*TR+(TJ=-OE)*TW)*-1
5220    IF CL=J1 AND DD>0GOTO5270
5230    DP=DP+N1
5240    IF CL=J1 THENGOTO5270
5250    CL=CL+DD
5260    GOTO5180
5270    IF CJ=1THENJA=JA+DD*DP+(DD>0)*-3:GOTO5310
5280    IF DD>ZE THEN DP=DP+2
5290    IF DP>126 ANDDD<ZE THENGOTO5460
5300    IF DP>129AND DD>ZE THENGOTO5460
5310    XQ$=MID$(C$(J,1),1,2):GOSUB10000:V=XQ
5320    POKEG,V:G=G+OE
5330    IF CJ=OE THENPOKEG,JA-INT(JA/QK)*QK:G=G+OE:POKEG,INT(JA/QK
        ):G=G+OE:GOTO5360
5340    IF DD<ZE THEN DP=256-DP
5345    IF DP=0 THEN DP=256
5350    DP=DP-TW:POKEG,DP:G=G+1
5360    PRINT "OK"
5370    GOTO5470
5380    FORI=1TO 5 STEP 2
5390    K=INT(I/TW+OE)
5400    XQ$=MID$(C$(J,K),1,2):GOSUB10000:V=XQ
5410    IF ER=1 OR V=-1 THENGOTO5440
5420    POKEG,V
5430    G=G+OE
5440    NEXT I
5450    GOTO5470
5460    PRINT"** ▲ ERROR-BRANCH ▲ OUT ▲ OF ▲ RANGE ▲ **"
5470    NEXTJ
5480    GOTO2020
6000    CO$=""
6010    REM ********DISEMBLE
6020    DC$="0000"
6030    INPUT"DISASSEMBLE ▲ FROM ▲ WHAT ▲ ADDRESS ▲ ";DM$
6035    XQ$=RIGHT$((DC$+DM$),4):GOSUB15000:IF ER=1 THEN 6030
6038    DM=XQ
6039    PRINT" ▄ DISASSEMBLING ▲ FROM ▲ ADDRESS ▲ $";XQ$
6040    G=DM:F=0:FM=0
6050    F=F+1:CO$=""
6060    FORI=1TO3
6070    V(I)=PEEK(G):H=INT(V(I)/16):L=V(I)-16*H
6080    R$(I)=MID$(D$,H+1,1)+MID$(D$,L+1,1)
6090    G=G+1:NEXTI
6100    FORI=1TOPC(V(1)+1):CO$=CO$+R$(I):NEXTI
6110    GOSUB30000
```

172

```
6115    ET=DM:GOSUB 40000:PRINTHB$;":  .  ";
6117    FOR I=1TOPC(Y)
6120    PRINT R$(I);"  .  ";
6130    NEXTI
6134    WW=15-(LEN(CO$)+PC(Y)):PRINTSPC(WW);DI$
6138    G=(G-3)+PC(Y):DM=G
6140    IF F<>22 THENGOTO6050
6150    GET K$:IF K$="" THEN 6150
6160    IF K$<>"M" THEN F=ZE:GOTO6050
6200    GOTO2020
7000    REM
7010    REM ********LOAD
7020    PRINT" .  "
7030    PRINT"LOAD  .  PROGRAM"
7035    INPUT"INPUT  .  FILENAME";N$
7037    IF N$="" THEN 7035
7040    OPEN1,1,0,N$
7041    T=0:FF=0
7045    FOR I=1TO200:CD$(I)="":J$(I)=""
7046    T=T+1
7047    GET#1,I$(I)
7048    IF I$(I)=CHR$(13)THEN FF=0:GOTO7058
7049    IF I$(I)="," THEN FF=1:GOTO7047
7050    IF FF=1 GOTO 7057
7051    IF I$(I)>CHR$(47) AND I$(I)<CHR$(58)ANDFF=0THEN J$(I)=J$(I
        )+I$(I):GOTO7047
7054    IF I$(I)="*" THEN 7059
7055    IF I$(I)="  .  " THEN 7047
7057    CD$(I)=CD$(I)+I$(I):GOTO7047
7058    NEXTI
7059    CLOSE1
7060    FOR I=1 TO T-1
7061    X(I)=VAL(J$(I)):Y=1
7062    FOR J=1TO3
7063    C$(X(I),J)=MID$(CD$(I),Y,2)
7066    C$(X(I),J)=LEFT$(C$(X(I),J)+"  .   .  ",2)
7067    Y=Y+2
7068    NEXT J:NEXT I
7069    FOR I=1 TO 200
7070    TP=I
7080    IF C$(I,1)<>"  .   .  "THEN7100
7090    NEXTI
7100    FORI=200TO1 STEP -1
7110    BP=I
7120    IF C$(I,1)<>"  .   .  "THEN7140
7130    NEXTI
7140    GOTO2020
8000    REM
8010    REM *********SAVE
8020    INPUT"ENTER  .  NAME  .  :  .  ";N$
8030    IF N$="" THEN 8020
8035    R$=","
8040    OPEN1,1,1,N$
8050    FORI=1TO200
8052    IF C$(I,1)="  .   .  "THEN 8080
8055    CO$=C$(I,1)+C$(I,2)+C$(I,3)
8060    PRINT#1,I;R$CO$
8080    NEXT I
8090    PRINT#1,"*":CLOSE1
```

173

```
8100    GOTO2020
9000    REM
9010    REM INITIALISATION
9020    ZE=0:OE=1:TW=OE+OE:TR=OE+TW:FR=TW+TW:QK=256:MR=2020:LN=200
9030    DIM A$(15),J$(200),X(200)
9040    TP=LN:BP=OE:REM LINE. BUFFER
9050    DIM C$(LN,TR),I$(1200)
9060    PRINT"▲ ▐ ▲ ▲ ▲ ▲ ▲ ▲ ▲ ▲ ▲ ▲ ▲ ▲ INITIALISI
        NG"
9070    FORI=OE TO LN
9080    FORJ=OE TO TR
9090    C$(I,J)=" ▲ ▲ "
9100    NEXTJ
9120    NEXT I
9125    DIM PC(256),DS$(256),R$(7),CD$(200),MQ(176)
9126    FOR A=1TO256:READ PC(A),DS$(A):NEXTA
9130    D$="0123456789ABCDEF"
9150    PRINT" ▐ "
9160    INPUT "LOCATE ▲ PROGRAM ▲ AT ▲ ADDRESS ▲ : ▲ ";XQ$:XQ$=
        LEFT$(XQ$+"0000",4)
9170    GOSUB15000:IF ER=1 OR XQ=0 THEN 9160
9175    R=XQ:POKER,0
9180    PRINT" ▐ "
9185    ET=R:GOSUB 40000
9190    PRINT"PROGRAM ▲ TO ▲ BE ▲ LOCATED ▲ AT ▲ ADDRESS ▲ $";HB$
9191    GOTO 2020
9198    REM ALL SPACES IN DATA STATEMENTS MUST BE TYPED IN
9199    DATA1,BRK,2,"ORA ▲ ($ ▲ ▲ ,X)",1,???,1,???,1,???,2,ORA $,
        2,ASL $,1,???
9200    DATA1,PHP,2,ORA #$,1,ASL A,1,???,1,???,3,ORA $,3,ASL $,1,?
        ??
9201    DATA2,"BPL ▲ "
9202    DATA2,"ORA ▲ ($ ▲ ▲ ),Y",1,???,1,???,1,???,2,"ORA ▲ $ ▲
        ▲ ,X",2,"ASL ▲ $ ▲ ▲ ,X"
9203    DATA1,???,1,CLC,3,"ORC ▲ $ ▲ ▲ ▲ ,Y",1,???,1,???,1,??
        ?,3,"ORA ▲ $ ▲ ▲ ,X"
9204    DATA3,"ASL ▲ $ ▲ ▲ ▲ ,X",1,???,3,JSR ,2,"AND ▲ ($ ▲
        ▲ ,X)",1,???,1,???,2,"BIT ▲ $"
9205    DATA2,AND $,2,ROL $,1,???,1,PLP,2,AND #$,1,ROL A,1,???,3,"
        BIT ▲ $"
9206    DATA3,AND $,3,ROL $,1,???,2,BMI $,2,"AND ▲ ($ ▲ ▲ ),Y"
9207    DATA1,???,1,???,1,???,2,"AND ▲ $ ▲ ▲ ,X"
9208    DATA2,"ROL ▲ $ ▲ ▲ ,X",1,???,1,SEC,3,"AND ▲ $ ▲ ▲ ▲ ▲
        ,Y",1,???,1,???,1,???
9209    DATA3,"AND ▲ $ ▲ ▲ ▲ ▲ ,X",3,"ROL ▲ $ ▲ ▲ ▲ ▲ ,X",1,
        ???,1,RTI,2,"EOR ▲ ($ ▲ ▲ ,X)",1,???
9210    DATA1,???,1,???,2,EOR $,2,LSR $,1,???,1,PHA,2,EOR #$,1,LSR
        A,1,???
9211    DATA3,JMP ,3,EOR $,3,LSR $,1,???,2,"BVC ▲ "
9212    DATA2,"EOR ▲ ($ ▲ ▲ ),Y",1,???
9213    DATA1,???,1,???,2,"EOR ▲ $ ▲ ▲ ,X",2,"LSR ▲ $ ▲ ▲ ,X",1,
        ???,1,CLI,3,"EOR ▲ $ ▲ ▲ ▲ ,Y"
9214    DATA1,???,1,???,1,???,3,"EOR ▲ $ ▲ ▲ ▲ ▲ ,X",3,"LSR ▲ $
        ▲ ▲ ▲ ▲ ,X",1,???,1,RTS
9215    DATA2,"ADC ▲ ($ ▲ ▲ ,X)",1,???,1,???,1,???,2,ADC $,2,ROR
        $,1,???,1,PLA
9313    DATA2,ADC #$,1,ROR A,1,???,3,JMP (,3,ADC $,3,ROR $,1,???
9314    DATA2,BVS ,2,"ADC ▲ ($ ▲ ▲ ),Y"
9315    DATA1,???,1,???,1,???,2,"ADC ▲ $ ▲ ▲ ,X",2,"ROR ▲ $ ▲ ▲
        ,X",1,???,1,"SEI"
```

174

```
9316 DATA3,"ADC ▲ $ ▲ ▲ ▲ ▲ ,Y",1,???,1,???,1,???,3,"ADC ▲ $
     ▲ ▲ ▲ ,X",3,"ROR ▲ $ ▲ ▲ ▲ ,X"
9317 DATA1,???,1,???,2,"STA ▲ ($ ▲ ▲ ,X)",1,???,1,???,2,STY $,
     2,STA $,2,"STX ▲ $"
9318 DATA1,???,1,DEY,1,???,1,TXA,1,???,3,STY $,3,STA $,3,STX $,
     1,???
9319 DATA2,BCC ,2,"STA ▲ ($ ▲ ▲ ,X)"
9320 DATA1,???,1,???,2,"STY ▲ $ ▲ ▲ ,X",2,"STA ▲ $ ▲ ▲ ,X"
9321 DATA2,"STX ▲ $ ▲ ▲ ,Y",1,???,1,TYA,3,"STA ▲ $ ▲ ▲ ▲
     ,Y"
9322 DATA 1,TXS,1,???,1,???,3,"STA ▲ $ ▲ ▲ ▲ ,X",1,???,1,?
     ??,2,"LDY ▲ #$"
9323 DATA2,"LDA ▲ ($ ▲ ▲ ,X)",2,LDX #$,1,???,2,LDY $,2,LDA $,2
     ,LDX $,1,???
9324 DATA 1,TAY,2,LDA #$,1,TAX,1,???,3,LDY $,3,LDA $,3,LDX $,1,
     ???
9325 DATA2,BCS ,2,"LDA ▲ ($ ▲ ▲ ),Y",1,???,1,???,2,"LDY ▲ $ ▲
     ▲ ,X",2,"LDA ▲ $ ▲ ▲ ,X"
9326 DATA2,"LDX ▲ $ ▲ ▲ ,Y",1,???,1,CLV,3,"LDA ▲ $ ▲ ▲ ▲
     ,Y",1,TSX,1,???,3,"LDY ▲ $ ▲ ▲ ▲ ,X"
9327 DATA3,"LDA ▲ $ ▲ ▲ ▲ ,X",3,"LDX ▲ $ ▲ ▲ ▲ ,Y",1,
     ???,2,CPY #$,2,"CMP ▲ ($ ▲ ▲ ,X)"
9329 DATA1,???,1,???,2,CPY $,2,CMP $,2,DEC $,1,???,1,INY,2,CMP
     #$,1,DEX
9331 DATA1,???,3,CPY $,3,CMP $,3,DEC $,1,???,2,"BNE ▲ ",2,"CMP
     ▲ ($ ▲ ▲ ),Y"
9333 DATA1,???,1,???,1,???,2,"CMP ▲ $ ▲ ▲ ,X",2,"DEC ▲ $ ▲ ▲
     ,X",1,???,1,CLD
9335 DATA3,"CMP ▲ $ ▲ ▲ ▲ ,Y",1,???,1,???,1,???,3,"CMP ▲ $
     ▲ ▲ ▲ ▲ ,X",3,"DEC ▲ $ ▲ ▲ ▲ ,X"
9337 DATA1,???,2,CPX #$,2,"SBC ▲ ($ ▲ ▲ ,X)",1,???,1,???,2,CPX
     $,2,"SBC ▲ $"
9339 DATA2,INC $,1,???,1,INX,2,SBC #$,1,NOP,1,???,3,CPX $,3,"SB
     C ▲ $"
9341 DATA3,INC $,1,???,2,BEQ ,2,"SBC ▲ ($ ▲ ▲ ),Y",1,???,1,???
     ,1,???
9343 DATA2,"SBC ▲ $ ▲ ▲ ,X",2,"INC ▲ $ ▲ ▲ ,X",1,???,1,SED,3,
     "SBC ▲ $ ▲ ▲ ▲ ,Y",1,???,1,???
9345 DATA1,???,3,"SBC ▲ $ ▲ ▲ ▲ ,X",3,"INC ▲ $ ▲ ▲ ▲
     ,X",1,???
10000 IFXQ$=""THEN XQ=-1:ER=1:RETURN
10005 AS=ASC(LEFT$(XQ$,1))-48:IFAS>22THEN ER=1:RETURN
10006 IF AS<10 AND AS>-1THEN GOTO 10010
10007 AS=AS-7:IF AS<10 THEN ER=1:RETURN
10010 XQ=ASC(RIGHT$(XQ$,1))-48:IFXQ>22THEN ER=1:RETURN
10016 IF XQ<10 AND XQ>-1THEN GOTO 10020
10017 XQ=XQ-7:IF XQ<10 THEN ER=1:RETURN
10020 XQ=XQ+16*AS:ER=0:RETURN
15000 QQ$=LEFT$(XQ$,2):QW$=RIGHT$(XQ$,2)
15005 XQ$=QQ$:GOSUB 10005:QQ=256*XQ
15007 IF ER=1 THEN RETURN
15010 XQ$=QW$:GOSUB 10005
15020 XQ=XQ+QQ:XQ$=QQ$+QW$
15030 RETURN
20000 JJ=(JJ$="90")+(JJ$="B0")+(JJ$="F0")+(JJ$="30")+(JJ$="D0")+
      (JJ$="10")
20010 JJ=(JJ+(JJ$="50")+(JJ$="70"))-((JJ$="4C")+(JJ$="6C")+(JJ$=
      "20"))
```

```
20020 RETURN
30000 XQ$=LEFT$(CO$,2):IFXQ$=" ▴ ▴ " THEN DI$="":RETURN
30001 FL=0:SH=0:ER=0
30002 GOSUB 10000:Y=XQ+1:XQ=0
30003 GOSUB 32000
30004 IF ER=2 AND FM=1 THEN30011
30005 IF ER>0ORXQ=-1THEN C$(J,1)=" ▴ ▴ ":RETURN
30010 JJ$=XQ$:GOSUB20000
30011 IF PC(Y)=1 THEN DI$=DS$(Y):RETURN
30015 DI$=LEFT$(DS$(Y),5)
30020 IF JJ<>0 THEN 30140
30030 IF RIGHT$(DI$,1)="("OR RIGHT$(DI$,1)="#" THENDI$=DI$+"$"
30040 IF PC(Y)=2 THEN DI$=DI$+RIGHT$(CO$,2)
30050 IF PC(Y)=3 THEN30090
30060 IF LEN(DS$(Y))=9 THEN DI$=DI$+RIGHT$(DS$(Y),2)
30070 IF LEN(DS$(Y))=11 THEN DI$=DI$+RIGHT$(DS$(Y),3)
30080 RETURN
30090 OP$=RIGHT$(CO$,2)+MID$(CO$,3,2)
30100 IF LEN(DS$(Y))=5 THEN DI$=DI$+OP$
30110 IF LEN(DS$(Y))=10 THEN DI$=DI$+OP$+RIGHT$(DS$(Y),1)
30120 IF LEN(DS$(Y))=11 THEN DI$=DI$+OP$+RIGHT$(DS$(Y),2)
30130 RETURN
30140 OP$=RIGHT$(CO$,2)+MID$(CO$,3,2)
30150 IF MID$(CO$,3,1)="L" THENDI$=DS$(Y)+RIGHT$(CO$,(LEN(CO$)-2
     )):SH=1
30157 IF JJ=1 AND FM=1 THEN DI$=DI$+OP$
30170 IF JJ=1 AND FM=0 AND SH=0 AND LEN(DS$(Y))=4THEN DI$=DI$+OP
     $
30175 IF JJ=1 AND FM=0 AND SH=0 AND LEN(DS$(Y))=5THEN DI$=DS$(Y)
     +OP$+")"
30180 IF JJ<>-1 OR FM<>1 THEN RETURN
30190 XQ$=RIGHT$(CO$,2):GOSUB 10000:ZZ=(G-3)+PC(Y)
30200 IF XQ>127 THEN XQ=-1*(256-XQ)
30210 ET=ZZ+XQ:GOSUB 40000
30220 DI$=DI$+HB$:RETURN
32000 IF ER=1 GOTO 32090
32010 IF DS$(Y)="???" THEN ER=2:GOTO32090
32020 IF LEN(CO$)<>PC(Y)*2 AND MID$(CO$,3,1)<>"L" THENER=3:GOTO3
     2090
32030 FORFI=2 TO LEN(CO$)
32040 IF MID$(CO$,3,1)="L" THEN 32080
32050 IF MID$(CO$,FI,1)<CHR$(48) THEN ER=4
32060 IF MID$(CO$,FI,1)>CHR$(57) AND MID$(CO$,FI,1)<CHR$(65)
     THEN ER=4
32070 IF MID$(CO$,FI,1)>CHR$(70) THEN ER=4
32080 NEXTFI
32090 RETURN
40000 HB$="":IF ET>65535 THEN ET=ET-65536:GOTO40000
40003 FORRR=3TO0STEP-1
40005 RT=INT(ET/(16^RR))
40010 ET=ET-RT*16^RR:RT=(RT+48)-7*(RT>9)
40015 HB$=HB$+CHR$(RT):NEXTRR
40070 RETURN
60000 REM **********CHEXSUM
60010 REM WARNING PROOF READ THIS SECTION
60020 REM CAREFULLY
62000 T=PEEK(62)*256+PEEK(61)+1
62010 INPUT"TO ▴ PRINTER ▴ (Y ▴ OR ▴ N ▴ ) ▴ ";Q$
62011 IF Q$<>"Y" THEN 62020
```

```
62015 CLOSE4,4:OPEN4,4:CMD4:PRINTCHR$(1);CHR$(129)
62020 PRINTCHR$(147);"CHECK _ SUM _ :-":LINK=PEEK(44)*256+PEEK(4
      3):E=62000
62100 REM****MAIN LOOP
62120 T=LINK
62130 LINK=PEEK(T+1)*256+PEEK(T)
62135 LN=PEEK(T+3)*256+PEEK(T+2)
62136 IF LN>E THEN PRINT:PRINT"TOTAL=";CH:CLOSE4,4:END
62137 S$=STR$(LN):L=LEN(S$)-1:S$=MID$(S$,2,L)
62138 PRINTSPC(6-L);S$;
62140 CS=0:N=0:C=0
62150 FORP=T+4 TO LINK-2:PK=PEEK(P)
62160 IF PK=143 THEN P=LINK-2:GOTO62190
62165 IF PK=34 THENC=(C=0)
62170 IF C=0 AND PK=32 THEN 62190
62180 IF PK=137 THENN=N+1:CS=CS+(2030RN):PK=164
62185 N=N+1:CS=CS+(PKORN)
62190 NEXTP:CH=CH+CS:PRINT"=";RIGHT$(STR$(CS),LEN(STR$(CS))-1):
      GOTO62120
62999 REM
```

CHECKSUM OUTPUT

(See Chapter 4 — To Get ALPA Running)

0=0	2010=0	2290=2075
100=0	2020=2495	2300=3491
110=0	2040=1555	2310=494
111=0	2042=3066	2320=420
112=0	2045=1559	2330=1943
115=0	2050=1122	2340=508
116=0	2060=1682	2350=2033
118=0	2065=4120	2360=2379
120=0	2067=4876	2370=1530
150=587	2070=1229	2380=1055
1000=0	2080=206	2385=1260
1010=0	2090=3066	2390=348
1020=0	2100=1058	2391=2141
1030=1231	2110=1524	2392=2157
1040=830	2120=510	2393=2815
1050=1259	2130=1008	2394=2162
1053=3484	2140=2895	2400=581
1054=2562	2150=206	2590=0
1055=402	2160=398	2600=3870
1056=921	2162=1743	2610=1420
1061=1063	2170=889	2620=1877
1062=1008	2180=1057	2630=1121
1069=523	2190=1225	2635=3854
1070=1692	2195=1837	2636=730
1071=587	2200=206	2640=3801
1075=3074	2210=1357	2641=241
1080=2047	2220=1172	2645=1121
1090=547	2230=1142	2650=3815
1095=679	2240=584	2655=730
1100=1278	2250=1349	2660=581
1110=205	2260=2388	2700=0
1120=143	2270=1501	2710=660
2000=0	2280=1364	2720=2308

177

```
2730=2999        5140=1474        6150=1293
2740=504         5150=868         6160=2048
2750=2386        5160=1313        6200=581
2755=397         5170=718         7000=0
2760=1957        5180=2469        7010=0
2765=1816        5190=1984        7020=372
2770=2320        5192=4156        7030=1157
2775=4464        5200=1900        7035=1508
2776=924         5210=3207        7037=924
2780=2654        5220=1785        7040=579
2785=2203        5230=793         7041=756
2789=970         5240=1390        7045=2197
2790=289         5250=793         7046=577
2795=1295        5260=592         7047=567
2800=2033        5270=3672        7048=2251
2810=581         5280=1553        7049=1992
3000=0           5290=2099        7050=1135
3005=1119        5300=2107        7051=5055
3010=0           5310=2330        7054=1156
3020=926         5320=1080        7055=1153
3030=1084        5330=6319        7057=2104
3040=1019        5340=1664        7058=206
3044=1927        5345=1223        7059=212
3046=1930        5350=2008        7060=919
3050=1080        5360=384         7061=1390
3060=1091        5370=585         7062=655
3070=1083        5380=889         7063=1755
3080=978         5390=1288        7066=2318
3090=1493        5400=2348        7067=587
3100=1087        5410=1885        7068=475
3110=1081        5420=355         7069=766
3115=1090        5430=644         7070=423
3119=1438        5440=206         7080=1440
3120=579         5450=585         7090=206
4000=0           5460=2542        7100=1167
4010=0           5470=205         7110=405
4020=1039        5480=581         7120=1444
4025=1191        6000=444         7130=206
4030=1231        6010=0           7140=581
4040=3662        6020=660         8000=0
4045=372         6030=2923        8010=0
4050=348         6035=2998        8020=1321
4060=581         6038=504         8030=912
5000=0           6039=2975        8035=421
5010=0           6040=1236        8040=580
5020=3924        6050=1079        8050=766
5040=876         6060=656         8052=1264
5050=1768        6070=3252        8055=2010
5060=2131        6080=2542        8060=716
5070=3118        6090=817         8080=206
5080=2585        6100=2912        8090=662
5090=4943        6110=402         8100=581
5095=2232        6115=1756        9000=0
5100=1675        6117=930         9010=0
5110=1830        6120=689         9020=5896
5120=1889        6130=206         9030=1306
5121=3555        6134=2748        9040=1129
5125=2654        6138=1655        9050=1199
5130=1871        6140=1464        9060=2164
```

```
9070=854          10005=3060        40005=1535
9080=873          10006=2145        40010=3461
9090=755          10007=2183        40015=1563
9100=205          10010=3090        40020=143
9120=206          10016=2181        60000=0
9125=2565         10017=2243        60010=0
9126=2104         10020=1847        60020=0
9130=1478         15000=2186        62000=1848
9150=372          15005=2041
9160=4503         15007=838         TOTAL= 681508
9170=2032         15010=1105
9175=839          15020=2004
9180=372          15030=143
9185=911          20000=6186
9190=3263         20010=5612
9191=581          20020=143
9198=0            30000=2771
9199=4003         30001=1336
9200=3625         30002=1624
9201=585          30003=402
9202=4057         30004=1572
9203=4014         30005=2539
9204=4388         30010=1088
9205=3956         30011=1928
9206=2792         30015=1156
9207=2039         30020=1171
9208=3725         30030=3407
9208=4539         30040=2364
9210=4178         30050=1190
9211=2395         30060=2931
9212=1315         30070=2993
9213=4796         30080=143
9214=4143         30090=1934
9215=4025         30100=2263
9313=3300         30110=3405
9314=1404         30120=3406
9315=3967         30130=143
9316=4306         30140=1934
9317=4458         30150=4406
9318=4008         30157=2305
9319=1406         30170=4207
9320=2558         30175=4750
9321=2671         30180=1979
9322=3720         30190=2932
9323=3850         30200=2238
9324=3674         30210=1392
9325=4132         30220=1121
8326=4960         32000=1197
9327=4081         32010=2289
9329=4244         32020=4527
9331=3949         32030=1162
9333=3805         32040=1635
9335=4346         32050=2125
9337=3967         32060=3929
9339=3951         32070=2118
9341=3337         32080=276
9343=4752         32090=143
9345=2682         40000=3238
10000=2056        40003=1151
```

179

Appendix 14
Screen Codes

Character Set 1	Character Set 2	Screen Code
∂		0
A	a	1
B	b	2
C	c	3
D	d	4
E	e	5
F	f	6
G	g	7
H	h	8
I	i	9
J	j	10
K	k	11
L	l	12
M	m	13
N	n	14
O	o	15
P	p	16
Q	q	17
R	r	18
S	s	19
T	t	20
U	u	21
V	v	22
W	w	23
X	x	24
Y	y	25
Z	z	26
[		27
£		28
]		29

Character Set 1	Character Set 2	Screen Code
↑		30
←		31
space		32
!		33
"		34
#		35
$		36
%		37
&		38
'		39
(		40
)		41
∗		42
+		43
,		44
—		45
.		46
/		47
0		48
1		49
2		50
3		51
4		52
5		53
6		54
7		55
8		56
9		57
÷		58
;		59
<		60
=		61
>		62
?		63
		64
♠	A	65
	B	66
	C	67
	D	68
	E	69

Character Set 1	Character Set 2	Screen Code
⬚	F	70
⬚	G	71
⬚	H	72
◩	I	73
◪	J	74
◨	K	75
⬚	L	76
◩	M	77
◪	N	78
⬚	O	79
⬚	P	80
■	Q	81
⬚	R	82
♥	S	83
⬚	T	84
◩	U	85
⊠	V	86
◙	W	87
✚	X	88
⬚	Y	89
◆	Z	90
⊞		91
◫		92
⬚		93
π	▩	94
◣	▨	95
space		96
◧		97
⬚		98
⬚		99
⬚		100
⬚		101
■		102
⬚		103
◪		104
◨	▨	105
⬚		106
◫		107
◪		108

183

Character Set 1	Character Set 2	Screen Code
◨		109
◪		110
▢		111
◩		112
◫		113
▦		114
◪		115
▢		116
◖		117
◗		118
▢		119
▤		120
▥		121
▢		122
◣		123
◤		124
◥		125
◢		126
◆		127

Codes 128-255 produce reversed images of codes 0-127

GLOSSARY

ASSEMBLER

This is a program which takes a program written in ASSEMBLY LANGUAGE, a form which the programmer can understand but which is meaningless to the microprocessor, and converts it to MACHINE CODE which the microprocessor can understand but which is difficult for the programmer to work with.

ASSEMBLY CODE

See ASSEMBLY LANGUAGE

ASSEMBLY LANGUAGE

This is a program written out in a form the programmer can understand but which means nothing directly to the MICROPROCESSOR until run through an ASSEMBLER. Any large MACHINE CODE program will be written via ASSEMBLY LANGUAGE (see ASSEMBLER).

BINARY

Base 2. Used by almost all computers. Each digit can have only two possible values — 0 and 1 (electrically on and off etc.). By making the possible value of the digit worth more depending on its position as we do in decimal etc.

$$145$$
$$= 1 \times 100 + 4 \times 10 + 5 \times 1$$

binary becomes etc.

$$1011$$
$$= 1 \times 8 + 0 \times 4 + 1 \times 2 + 1 \times 1 = 11 \text{ decimal}$$

BIT

One BINARY digit, which can only take the value of a one or a zero. When strung together it can be used to form a larger number (see BINARY, see BYTE).

BUFFER

An area of memory set aside for temporary storage of data. Usually used in relation to input/output functions.

BYTE

The basic unit of the computer's MEMORY. One MEMORY LOCATION can hold 1 BYTE of information. Each BYTE is made up of 8 BITS and can store a number between 0 and 255. This number may represent a character, a numeric value, or part of a microprocessor instruction. Can be strung together like BITS to form larger numbers (see BINARY).

CHARACTER

Generally any symbol which can be put on the screen by pressing a key on the keyboard. Any symbol (alphanumeric) you can write (that is not a drawing or a picture) is a CHARACTER. NOTE: for an exception see GRAPHICS CHARACTERS.

CHARACTER SET

The set of all CHARACTERS which can be printed on the TEXT screen.

DECIMAL

Base 10. Our normal everyday way of counting is called the decimal number system.

DISASSEMBLER

A program which takes a MACHINE CODE program and prints it out in ASSEMBLY LANGUAGE so the programmer can read it (see ASSEMBLER).

DUMP

A memory DUMP is a display of the contents of memory in a numerical or character form (not as ASSEMBLY CODE instructions).

GRAPHICS

In GRAPHICS mode you can display anything on the screen that you can display using the resolution of the dots the computer puts out (the size of a full stop).

GRAPHICS CHARACTER

Part of the CHARACTER SET is made up of CHARACTERS which are only shapes and hold no symbolic meaning. These are GRAPHICS CHARACTERS.

HEXADECIMAL

Base 16 (sometimes called HEX). Base 16 is used in dealing with machine code because it is an easy way of dealing with BINARY numbers, which very soon become cumbersome. A BYTE is divided into two sections of four binary BITS, each capable of storing a number from

187

$\emptyset \rightarrow 15$. The number is represented by a HEX digit $\emptyset \rightarrow 9$, $A \rightarrow F$. Thus a byte can be displayed by using two HEX digits. A **$** sign is usually used to signify a HEX number.

INTERRUPT

An interrupt is an electronic signal sent to the microprocessor, by a peripheral or a chip within the computer, to notify it of something happening in the outside world.

MACHINE CODE

Sometimes called MACHINE LANGUAGE, it is the way of describing a program that can be directly run by the MICROPROCESSOR. A MACHINE CODE program is made up of a string of numbers which may be put into the computer by the programmer in HEX, or assembled using an ASSEMBLER from a program written in ASSEMBLY CODE.

MACHINE LANGUAGE

See MACHINE CODE.

MEMORY

Boxes at pigeonholes within the computer which are used to hold numbers, machine language instructions and characters. Each box can hold only 1 BYTE of memory at a time. The C64 has 64K (65536) bytes of memory.

MEMORY ADDRESS

Each memory box has a number from $\emptyset$ to 65535 which is used to refer to it from among the 65536 within the computer. A number used for this purpose is called an address.

MEMORY LOCATION

An easier way of saying memory at address.

MICROPROCESSOR

The central processing and control unit of the computer. It can be compared to the human brain (as long as you realise that the brain is of comparatively immense power with huge memory and enormously complex programs). The microprocessor controls all movement of data, all decisions and all calculations within the computer.

TEXT

In TEXT mode you can only display CHARACTERS which are in the CHARACTER SET on the screen (see GRAPHICS).

VECTOR

Is the name given to bytes in RAM which store the address of a ROM routine. These bytes are used so that the process of the operating system or basic calling ROM input/output routines may be accessed by the user. The progammer will set these RAM bytes to point to his own program to handle input/output in his own way.

ZERO PAGE

Another name for the first 356 bytes of memory from $0 to $255.

Index

Absolute addressing 9, 17, 21, 40
Accumulator 7-8
Addition 32
Addition two byte 34
Addresses 4
Addressing modes 8, 55, 69, 103
ALPA 25
ALPA check sum 26, 182
ALPA commands 27
ALPA continuing with program intact 44
ALPA line number addressing 41
ALPA memory usage 29
ALPA program 169
ALPA starting 25
ALPA working with 26
AND 77, 78
Animation 40
ASL 81
Assembler 11, 187
Assembly language 11, 187

BASIC memory usage 143, 149
BASIC routines 160
BCC 47, 71
BCD 72
BCS 47, 71
BEQ 45, 71
Binary 17, 187
Bitmap mode 125
Bits 21, 77, 80
BMI 73, 76
BNE 46, 71
Boolean operations 77
Borrow 36
BPL 73, 76
Branches 44, 45, 47, 88
Break 71
BRK 71, 92
BVC 76
BVS 76
Byte 11

Calling a program 5
Carry flag 31, 46, 71
Character 188
Character generation ROM 62, 63, 119, 127
Character mode 124
Character set 12, 62, 63, 127, 188
CIA interface chip 137
CLC 71
CLD 72
CLI 72, 96
Clock 139
CLV 76
CMP 44, 46
Colour 122, 123
Colour memory 64
Colour mix chart 126

Colour values 126
Comparisons 44
Converting binary to hexidecimal 19
Converting hexidecimal to decimal 22, 115
Counters 54
Counting 51, 52

Debugging 71
DEC 52
Decimal 189
Decimal flag 72
Disassembler 189
Division 83
Dump 189

Efficiency 14, 46, 85
Entering a program 10
EOR 77, 80
Extended background colour mode 125

Flags 44, 71, 113

Go to 40
Graphics 61, 122, 189
Graphics character 189
Graphics finishing 66
Graphics memory 62, 64
Greater than 47

Hexadecimal 17, 189
Horizontal scroll 123

Immediate addressing 9
INC 52
Index 193
Index register 53, 56, 61
Indexed addressing 55
Indexed indirect addressing 68
Indirect addressing 69
Indirect indexed addressing 67
Infinite loops 43
Instruction set 103
Interrupt 190
Interrupts 71, 72, 92, 95
Interrupt flag 72
Inverting bits 80

JMP 87
Joystick 137
JSR 88
Jump 40
Jump conditional 44

Kernal 95
Kernal memory usage 143, 149
Kernal routines 149
Keyboard input 97, 137, 167

LDA 8
Less than 47

Mastering the Commodore 64

Mark Greenshields

C64

COMMODORE 64
GAMES BOOK 2

GREGG BARNETT

RS232 139
RTI 96
RTS 6, 88, 90

SBC 36
Screen chip 39, 121
Screen codes 165
Screen display code 12
Screen height 122
Screen memory 11, 39, 121
Screen modes 124
Screen width 123
Scroll — vertical 122
Scrolling 65
Searching memory 56
SEC 33, 71
SED 72
SEI 72, 96
Serial I/O 139, 140
Shifting bits 81
Signed arithmetic 73
Sound 128
Speed 3
Sprites 39, 121, 123
Sprite collisions 124
Sprite position chart 127
STA 9, 10
Stack 89, 90, 91, 92
Stack pointer 90, 92
Status byte 44, 71
Status register 103, 113
Subroutines 3, 88, 90
Subtraction 35
Switching memory blocks 119
SYS 4, 6

Tables 61, 67
Tables — zero pages 68
Text 191
Timer 140
Truth tables 77-78
TSY 92
Turning bits off 78
Turning bits on 79
Twos complement arithmetic 73, 117
TXS 92

Vectoring 69
Vectors 95, 191
VIC-II chips 39, 121
Video bank 121

X-registers 53, 56

Y-registers 53, 56

Zero flag 45, 46, 71
Zero page 191
Zero page addressing 9, 22
Zero page indexed addressing 59

Light pen 123, 137
Logical operations 77
Looping 51, 52
LSR 83

Machine code 11
Machine language 5
Masks 78
Mathematics 31
Memory 4, 190
Memory address 190
Memory contents 5
Memory location 191
Memory map 119
Memory uses 14
Memory usage 143
Memory usage — numbers 17
Machine code instructions 8
Microprocessor 191
Mnemonics 6, 11
Moving memory 7, 54
Multicolour bitmap mode 125
Multicolour character mode 124
Multiplication 51, 81, 83
Multiply two byte 82
Music 128

Negative flag 73
Negative numbers 73, 117
NOP 98
Numbers 31

Operating system 95
Operating system routines 149
ORA 77, 79
Overflow flag 75

Paddle buttons 137
Peek 5
PHA 91
Picking up memory 8
Pixel 61
PLA 91
Poke 5
Printing 12
Printing a message 13
Printing on graphics 61
Processor status code register 44, 71
Program counter 87
Putting things in memory 9

Raster register 123
Registers 7, 53
Register 5, 113
Register to register transfers 68
Relative addressing 45, 47, 117
Relocation 48
Return 5
Return address 89
ROL 82
Rotating bits 81
ROR 83